Mitigating Risk That Climate Change Poses to the National Critical Functions

Strategies for Supply Chains, Insurance Services, Emergency Management, and Public Safety

SUSAN A. RESETAR, ANDREW LAULAND, MICHELLE E. MIRO, JAY BALAGNA, R. J. BRIGGS, LIISA ECOLA, JESSICA JENSEN, BENJAMIN LEE PRESTON, KRISTIN J. LEUSCHNER

T0244368

HOMELAND SECURITY
OPERATIONAL ANALYSIS CENTER

About This Report

Climate change creates both risks and opportunities associated with ensuring the security and resilience of the services provided by the United States' critical infrastructure systems. These systems can be examined through the lens of the National Critical Functions (NCFs)— that is,

> functions of government and the private sector so vital to the United States that their disruption, corruption, or dysfunction would have a debilitating effect on security, national economic security, national public health or safety, or any combination thereof.[1]

The NCFs also provide a point of focus for understanding risk mitigation and climate adaptation options that can be implemented in response to risks to critical infrastructure. This report provides the results of an analysis of risk mitigation and climate adaptation options that can be implemented for four NCFs that had been identified in other parts of this research as being at risk of disruption on a national scale from climate change: *Maintain Supply Chains, Provide Insurance Services, Prepare for and Manage Emergencies,* and *Provide Public Safety.*[2] The information in this report will be of interest to a variety of infrastructure stakeholders with responsibility for anticipating climate change risks and for planning and implementing risk mitigation policies and practices.

This research was sponsored by the Cybersecurity and Infrastructure Security Agency's National Risk Management Center and conducted in the Infrastructure, Immigration, and Security Operations Program of the RAND Homeland Security Research Division, which operates the Homeland Security Operational Analysis Center (HSOAC).

About the Homeland Security Operational Analysis Center

The Homeland Security Act of 2002 (Public Law 107-296, § 305, as codified at 6 U.S.C. § 185) authorizes the Secretary of Homeland Security, acting through the Under Secretary for Science and Technology, to establish one or more federally funded research and development centers (FFRDCs) to provide independent analysis of homeland security issues. The RAND Corporation operates HSOAC as an FFRDC for the U.S. Department of Homeland Security (DHS) under contract 70RSAT22D00000001.

The HSOAC FFRDC provides the government with independent and objective analyses and advice in core areas important to the department in support of policy development,

---

[1] Cybersecurity and Infrastructure Security Agency, "National Critical Functions," undated.

[2] Lauland et al., *Strategies to Mitigate the Risk to the National Critical Functions Generated by Climate Change.*

decisionmaking, alternative approaches, and new ideas on issues of significance. HSOAC also works with and supports other federal, state, local, tribal, and public- and private-sector organizations that make up the homeland security enterprise. HSOAC's research is undertaken by mutual consent with DHS and organized as a set of discrete tasks. This report presents the results of research and analysis conducted under task order 770RCSA22FR0000028, Climate Change EO 14008. The results presented in this report do not necessarily reflect official DHS opinion or policy.

For more information on the RAND Homeland Security Research Division, see www.rand.org/hsrd. For more information on this publication, see www.rand.org/t/RRA1645-9.

Acknowledgments

We thank our peer reviewers, Christy Foran and Debra Knopman, of the RAND Corporation, whose thoughtful reviews helped to strengthen our findings and communicate them more clearly.

Summary

Climate change poses risks to communities throughout the United States, and these risks are projected to increase for decades into the future, with significant implications for infrastructure planning, investment, and operations, including the 55 National Critical Functions (NCFs). The NCFs represent

> functions of government and the private sector so vital to the United States that their disruption, corruption, or dysfunction would have a debilitating effect on security, national economic security, national public health or safety, or any combination thereof.[1]

Climate risk mitigation strategies are intended to reduce an NCF's vulnerability to, or the consequences from, the direct and indirect effects of climate change. These strategies can include activities to avoid exposure to the sources of climate risk (climate drivers); limit the physical damage, workforce consequences, or demand changes resulting from exposure; or buffer against cascading effects from disruption to other NCFs. These strategies are essentially what climate scientists refer to as *climate adaptation strategies*; they do not aim to reduce the likelihood of climate change and its effects but instead seek to provide options for incremental risk reduction in the short term and potentially transformative approaches in the long term.

This report is intended to inform risk mitigation planning and decisionmaking by contextualizing climate risk mitigation through a review of mitigation strategies for four NCFs: *Maintain Supply Chains*, *Provide Insurance Services*, *Prepare for and Manage Emergencies*, and *Provide Public Safety*. We selected these NCFs because they (1) rely on varying amounts of infrastructure and personnel to function and (2) have moderate or higher risk of disruption from climate change assessed at the national scale by 2100 using the current emissions scenario.[2] Some of these NCFs also have high potential to cascade risk onto other NCFs. The current study builds on the research team's previous work to examine climate risk mitigation options for the NCFs.

---

[1] Cybersecurity and Infrastructure Security Agency, "National Critical Functions," undated.

[2] Miro et al., "Assessing Risk to National Critical Functions as a Result of Climate Change." Risk ratings are assigned on a scale of 1 to 5 based on the amount of anticipated disruption at the national scale, with 1 being no disruption or normal operations and 5 being critical. To be at moderate risk of disruption at the national scale, an NCF would have to be expected to experience effects to routine operations over a large geographic area but remain operational in most of the country.

Approach

For each of the four NCFs, we drew on the policy and academic literature and our subject-matter expertise to answer a set of questions to understand the "ecosystem" in which the NCF operates and to identify practicable and effective approaches for mitigating the risks from climate change:

- Who are the actors responsible for climate risk mitigation for this NCF?
- What kinds of climate risk mitigation strategies are currently being pursued?
- What are the enablers and barriers to these strategies?
- Are there gaps in the risk areas in which there are few strategies or options to mitigate risk?
- What might be needed for transformative change?

Key Findings

As a group, these four NCFs offer insights into how to think about the challenges of risk mitigation:

- *Maintain Supply Chains* is a complex and widespread NCF with no singular actor or geographic concentration but with many potential choke points for disruption. This reality makes risk mitigation a diffuse activity that is difficult to centralize or assess for efficacy.
- *Prepare for and Manage Emergencies* and *Provide Public Safety* are two personnel-heavy functions with a high degree of activity at local levels: Local emergency responders and public safety officials are on the front lines of dealing with the effects of climate change. This fact means that risk mitigation must address the diverse needs of localities to meet the challenges resulting from more-frequent or severer climate drivers in the future.
- Mitigating risk for *Provide Insurance Services* depends both on direct activities to shore up vulnerabilities in the insurance market and on indirect activities that mitigate insurance-covered risks, such as flooding and hurricanes.
- Notably, these four NCFs can also be affected by community preparedness and hazard mitigation investments that might be implemented by other NCFs' stakeholders, a fact that exemplifies how risk mitigation investments in upstream NCFs can generate dividends to other NCFs.
- In addition, the latter three NCFs—*Provide Insurance Services, Prepare for and Manage Emergencies*, and *Provide Public Safety*—are not as widely covered in the climate adaptation literature and do not have significant asset footprints, and this fact suggests the need for a deeper understanding of these sectors' climate risk mitigation requirements.

Key Takeaways

In this section, we describe the key takeaways that can be derived from our examination of risk mitigation among this group of NCFs.

The NCF framework can be a useful lens for considering climate adaptation. The framework indicates how sources of climate risk (climate drivers) affect each NCF's routine operations, and understanding these effects provides insights into how to target vulnerabilities for climate risk mitigation. Traditional approaches to critical infrastructure are focused on physical assets. Applying the functional lens of the NCF framework allows communities to have a more comprehensive understanding of how climate risk can manifest and helps them identify and prioritize the functions most necessary to sustain a community. It also expands the potential set of climate adaptation strategies. For example, in addition to addressing risk to physical assets, the use of the NCF framework suggests adaptation measures that are related primarily to changing the underlying demand for a function (e.g., adaptation by individual property owners) or addressing considerations related to the workforce that provides it (e.g., national volunteer auxiliaries). This more comprehensive focus provides additional options for mitigating risk to the most-basic and -essential functions of a community while considering (but not being limited to) the physical assets associated with their provision. Additionally, the structure of the framework enables consideration of interdependencies among NCFs, which illustrate how risk can propagate through the entire set of NCFs. These sources of risk must also be mitigated, but, in some cases, the actors that mitigate these risks are only a subset of those stakeholders who could benefit from the mitigation action.

Data are often insufficient to provide insights into system risks for specific localities. A comprehensive understanding of an NCF's risk profile is critical to developing effective mitigation strategies. However, more data on the functional and geospatial relationships among the NCFs are needed to support a more complete understanding of an NCF's risk profile and to help better prioritize investments in risk mitigation. For example, lack of transparency across a supply chain makes *Maintain Supply Chains* vulnerable to extended disruptions. Incorporating data, such as information provided by blockchain technology, into a supply chain reduces risk because it provides a set of data about all links within a supply chain that any of the users can access.

Mitigating indirect risk to an NCF could be as effective as (or more effective than) mitigating direct risk to the NCF itself. For example, although direct risk from climate change is a significant source of risk to *Provide Public Safety*, this NCF is also at considerable risk from climate change–related disruption to other NCFs, such as *Distribute Electricity*. Here is one illustration: Hurricanes Irma and Maria damaged Puerto Rico's entire energy grid, which resulted in cascading disruptions to transportation, communications, water supply, stormwater management, hospitals, key archival storage facilities, and wastewater treatment facilities. Given the limited number of options to mitigate direct risk from climate change to the *Provide Public Safety* NCF and the importance of *Distribute Electricity* to it and to a large number of other NCFs, a more effective use of resources might be to attempt to mitigate risk to *Distribute Electricity*. This scenario is likely to apply to several NCFs and suggests that a wide array of entities might be able to reduce risk to any given NCF and that more-diverse policy options might be available than might initially appear to be the case given the structure of the NCF.

Better-coordinated and -targeted mitigation efforts are needed to reduce risk. Because each NCF involves multiple actors—each with its own roles, responsibilities, and priorities—current risk mitigation activities are often diffuse and uncoordinated. Coordinated efforts among regional, state, or local governments and nonprofits targeted at priority climate risks might be more impactful in reducing those risks. Some entities, such as the Cybersecurity and Infrastructure Security Agency or other federal actors, could have an important role in convening or facilitating such coordination and priority-setting. Existing climate collaboratives can be models for such efforts.

More-transformative risk mitigation efforts need to account for policy and systemic vulnerabilities, including cascading effects. Although risk mitigation actions focused on short-term or incremental change can be viable, no NCF exists in a vacuum, and mitigating risk on a larger or transformative scale means dealing with broader issues related to policy and systemic vulnerabilities, including cascading effects from other NCFs. For example, for *Provide Insurance Services*, both insurers and state and local governments can deploy strategies that support the actions of property owners and their communities and mitigate climate change's consequences for insurance markets overall. However, this possibility depends on the risk behavior of individuals, the capacity of *Provide Housing*, and people's willingness to invest in risk reduction for their own properties. Additionally, some solutions might be most effective when implemented at the federal scale or might require a portfolio approach to address systemic risks or avoid maladaptation.

Contents

Tables

CHAPTER 1

Background and Objectives

Introduction

Climate change poses risks to people and their communities throughout the United States. Scientific evidence indicates that climate change is already contributing to increases in the frequency and intensity of some types of extreme weather events. Risks associated with such extreme events are projected to increase for decades into the future, with significant implications for infrastructure planning, investment, and operations and for the National Critical Functions (NCFs). The NCFs represent

> functions of government and the private sector so vital to the United States that their disruption, corruption, or dysfunction would have a debilitating effect on security, national economic security, national public health or safety, or any combination thereof.[1]

Climate risk mitigation strategies are intended to reduce an NCF's vulnerability to, or the consequences from, the effects of climate change. In this report, we focus on how to mitigate risks to four NCFs: *Maintain Supply Chains*, *Provide Insurance Services*, *Prepare for and Manage Emergencies*, and *Provide Public Safety*.[2] For each of the four NCFs, the report provides an overview of the actors involved in providing the function; describes key climate risks, risk mitigation opportunities, and implementation experience; and gives illustrative examples of risk mitigation options. Each case includes strategies and options that various stakeholders or actors can implement to address climate risk. The information provided for

---

[1] Cybersecurity and Infrastructure Security Agency (CISA), "National Critical Functions," undated.

[2] Another report for this project identifies climate risk mitigation strategies for 25 NCFs that were assessed to be at least at moderate risk of disruption from climate change on a national scale. An NCF being at risk on a national scale implies that serious disruption to routine operations will occur for a period over a large geographic area. Effects at the local or regional level could be severer than what is indicated by a national rating. That report contains strategies that could be implemented specifically by owner-operators for each climate driver–impact mechanism pathway that exhibits moderate-level risk of disruption at a national scale. This analysis expands the options to include other types of stakeholders. All stakeholders must consider such issues as cost, feasibility, effectiveness, and unintended consequences when prioritizing, selecting, and implementing these strategies (Lauland et al., *Strategies to Mitigate the Risk to the National Critical Functions Generated by Climate Change*).

each NCF is intended to contextualize climate risk mitigation to drive risk mitigation planning and decisionmaking.

The information in this report will be of value to a broad array of infrastructure and operational stakeholders with responsibility for anticipating climate change risks and for planning and implementing risk mitigation policies and practices (Box 1.1). With different stakeholders having varying levels of climate change expertise and capacity for analysis, this report

---

BOX 1.1

Potential Stakeholders and Applications of the National Critical Function Risk Assessment Framework for Climate Change Analysis and Risk Mitigation

The NCFs provide valuable information to government and the private sector regarding drivers and consequences associated with the "disruption, corruption, or dysfunction"[a] of U.S. infrastructure and its operations. By design, the NCFs are intended to provide an approach to critical functions that is nationally consistent and relevant to a wide variety of government and industry users with responsibility for emergency management, hazard mitigation planning, and disaster response and recovery. However, each potential infrastructure stakeholder has unique information needs, as well as management authority and responsibility. The chart below presents five types of stakeholders representing key audiences for the NCFs and associated analytic products. Each stakeholder group is defined by a distinct mission area, as well as a distinct set of applications.

Stakeholder Type	Mission	Application of NCF Risk Assessments
National Risk Management Center analyst	Plan, analyze, and collaborate on strategic risk-reduction efforts for U.S. infrastructure.	• Enhancing operational tools and analyses for infrastructure risk assessment • Screening NCFs to identify at-risk functions • Maintaining cross-function situational awareness of potential threat drivers and risks of disruption • Identifying interdependent functions • Identifying leading indicators of NCF disruption • Identifying cost-effective risk mitigation options aligned to CISA's mission • Communicating infrastructure risks to government and private-sector stakeholders
Sector-specific risk management agency personnel	Provide knowledge and expertise for a critical infrastructure sector, and lead, facilitate, or support programs and associated activities relevant to maintaining the operation of that sector.	• Providing, supporting, or facilitating technical assistance regarding sector vulnerabilities and risk mitigation • Providing sector-specific critical infrastructure information on assets, vulnerabilities, and risk mitigation • Communicating infrastructure risks to government and private-sector stakeholders

Box 1.1—Continued

Stakeholder Type	Mission	Application of NCF Risk Assessments
CISA regional personnel	Provide cybersecurity, physical infrastructure security, chemical security, and emergency communication services to critical infrastructure partners at the regional, state, county, tribal, and local levels.	• Advising regional partners on potential threats to infrastructure functions and priority risks • Advising regional partners on cost-effective risk mitigation options • Training regional partners on the NCF framework and its application • Communicating infrastructure risks to regional government and private-sector stakeholders
Federal or SLTT emergency manager	Protect communities by coordinating activities that build, sustain, and improve the capability to mitigate against, prepare for, respond to, and recover from disasters.	• Identifying infrastructure vulnerabilities to climate variability and change • Prioritizing climate change–related risks relative to other hazards and associated risks • Identifying interdependent infrastructure systems and functions that enhance or reduce risk • Identifying, assessing, and implementing cost-effective asset management and risk mitigation options • Communicating risks to infrastructure assets and functions to government and private-sector stakeholders
Asset owner or operator	Own, manage, and operate infrastructure assets and their associated functions on behalf of public and private stakeholders.	• Making decisions about infrastructure investment and divestment • Planning and designing infrastructure projects • Understanding threats and associated risks to infrastructure assets and functions • Identifying, assessing, and implementing cost-effective asset management and risk mitigation options • Communicating infrastructure risks to government and private-sector stakeholders

NOTE: SLTT = state, local, tribal, or territorial.

[a] CISA, "National Critical Functions."

In using the NCFs to assess the impacts that climate change risk could have on U.S. infrastructure, analysts should consider the relevance of different types of information to each of these stakeholders. Such considerations include which stakeholders are responsible for different types of infrastructure functions and what mitigation strategies fall within the authority and responsibility of a given stakeholder group. In so doing, NCF analysts can enhance the value of analytic products to stakeholders.

provides a useful entry point for stakeholders by offering access to authoritative information on potential risk mitigation strategies that are specific to different infrastructure functions.

Analytic Approach

In the current analysis, we leveraged our recent assessment of climate risk to the 55 NCFs, in which we identified the anticipated level of disruption from eight climate drivers and four mechanisms through which these drivers would affect NCF assets and routine operations.[3] Four NCFs were selected for this review based on a variety of considerations, including priorities articulated by CISA. To draw attention to the full range of climate risks that need to be mitigated, we purposely sought to include NCFs that might rely on large amounts of infrastructure or those that rely more heavily on personnel to function. We considered NCFs that have moderate or higher risk of disruption from climate change assessed at a national scale by 2100 using the current emissions scenario.[4] As shown in Table 1.1, some of these NCFs also have high potential to cascade risk onto other NCFs (although we do not have detailed

TABLE 1.1
National Critical Functions Covered in This Report

NCF	Risk Rating for 2050	Risk Rating for 2100	Number of Downstream NCFs[a]
Maintain Supply Chains	4	5	54
Provide Insurance Services	2	4	Not applicable
Prepare for and Manage Emergencies	3	3	54
Provide Public Safety	3	3	19

NOTE: Risk ratings are assigned on a scale of 1 to 5 based on the amount of anticipated disruption at the national scale, with 1 being no disruption or normal operations and 5 being critical, in 2050 and in 2100. To be at moderate risk of disruption at the national scale, an NCF would have to be expected to experience effects to routine operations over a large geographic area but remain operational in most of the country. Risk ratings shown here reflect Homeland Security Operational Analysis Center researchers' risk assessment under a current emissions scenario (see Miro et al., *Assessing Risk to National Critical Functions as a Result of Climate Change*).

[a] This is the number of other NCFs that rely on outputs from the given NCF. These numbers indicate the numbers of relationships only. Characterizing the strength of these dependencies could lead to a more complete understanding of the ways in which climate drivers could disrupt operations for the network of NCFs and might illuminate points of intervention for reducing these risks.

---

[3] The eight climate drivers are flooding, sea-level rise, tropical cyclones and hurricanes, severe storm systems (nontropical), extreme cold, extreme heat, wildfire, and drought. *Tropical cyclone* is the broadest term and includes tropical depressions, tropical storms, and hurricanes, each of which is characterized by progressively stronger wind speeds.

[4] Miro et al., *Assessing Risk to National Critical Functions as a Result of Climate Change*.

information on the features of each of the downstream relationships that would affect how impacts to one NCF might propagate to others).[5] Additionally, although *Maintain Supply Chains* includes an expansive infrastructure footprint, the other three NCFs are not as rooted in physical infrastructure for their operations, providing a different lens through which to view climate risk mitigation.

The climate risk mitigation strategies described in this report are intended to reduce an NCF's vulnerability to, or the consequences from, both the direct and indirect effects of climate change. These strategies can include activities to avoid exposure to climate drivers; limit the physical damage, workforce consequences, or demand changes resulting from exposure; or buffer against cascading effects from disruption to other NCFs. For example, strategies might include moving assets away from areas where flooding might occur, hardening structures to withstand high winds, improving community preparedness and resilience to limit demand for assistance after an event, or diversifying a supplier base. These are essentially what climate scientists refer to as *climate adaptation strategies*, which are not the same as climate mitigation strategies, which are adopted to reduce the likelihood of climate change and its effects (although these distinctions can be blurred).[6] Although the impacts of climate change are affecting communities in the United States and around the world, the extent of this change and the effects at a specific location can be uncertain. Therefore, the strategies presented here might have to be adjusted as climate change effects progress over time. Although some strategies would be appropriate regardless of the amount of change, when there is considerable uncertainty around the amount of change, it is prudent to implement flexible or adaptable strategies and monitor their effectiveness over time, adjusting as more information becomes available. For example, seawalls, which can reduce storm surge effects, can be designed to be raised incrementally as sea levels rise.[7] There are strategies that provide incremental reduction to risks in the shorter term, but, for the longer term, as the effects of climate change become severer and more pronounced, more-transformative approaches might be necessary to realize substantial risk reduction.[8]

Each NCF operates in its own "ecosystem" that determines what approaches are practicable and effective for mitigating risks from climate change. Drawing on our review of the

---

[5] An NCF has a downstream dependence if a subfunction or an output of that NCF affects another NCF in some way.

[6] Climate mitigation strategies include reducing emissions of greenhouse gases, sequestering carbon in forested and other lands, and transforming energy and transportation systems to reduce dependencies on fossil fuels.

[7] Miami-Dade County, *Miami-Dade County Sea Level Rise Strategy*, p. 172.

[8] Deubelli and Mechler, "Perspectives on Transformational Change in Climate Risk Management and Adaptation."

policy and academic literature and our subject-matter expertise, we address the following questions in each chapter:

- Who are the actors responsible for climate risk mitigation for this NCF?
- What kinds of climate risk mitigation strategies are currently being pursued?
- What are the enablers and barriers to these strategies?
- Are there gaps in the risk areas in which there are few strategies or options to mitigate risk?
- What might be needed for transformative change?

For each NCF, we selected an illustrative set of climate risk mitigation strategies that address the most-significant impact pathways (the climate driver–mechanism combination) and were discussed in the literature as being effective measures. A discussion of enablers and barriers provides some indication of how feasible these strategies might be for the responsible parties to implement.

Study Limitations

This approach has some key limitations. The information contained in this report is a high-level synthesis of what is known about climate risk mitigation for the four identified NCFs. However, local conditions will ultimately dictate what is feasible and practical for risk mitigation and the status of actions to date. An NCF could be provided by a very heterogeneous group of actors and stakeholders with varying levels of financial and technical resources, information on climate drivers, and spans of management control and in locations or communities that have different needs and capacities. Therefore, the broad generalizations provided in this report might not be relevant for every actor or community.

The examples of climate risk mitigation strategies for each of the NCFs are derived from information available in the open literature. There might be proprietary methods not described in open sources that could also be effective. Nor are the examples provided in each chapter all-inclusive of the options available; rather, we selected them using the analysts' knowledge of the field to provide representative examples that address the primary sources of risk to an NCF.

Organization of This Report

The rest of this report is laid out as follows:

- Chapter Two describes climate risk mitigation for *Maintain Supply Chains.*
- Chapter Three describes climate risk mitigation for *Provide Insurance Services.*
- Chapter Four describes climate risk mitigation for *Prepare for and Manage Emergencies.*

- Chapter Five describes climate risk mitigation for *Provide Public Safety.*
- Chapter Six offers our conclusions and recommended next steps.

CHAPTER 2

Maintain Supply Chains

National Critical Function Overview and Risk Due to Climate Change

Description of the National Critical Function

CISA defines *Maintain Supply Chains* as follows: "Manage and sustain the networks of assets, systems, and relationships that enable the movement of goods and services from producers to consumers."[1] This NCF covers all elements of producing, transporting, distributing, and selling goods, regardless of the type of goods or their origin and destination. CISA breaks this NCF into six subfunctions:

- *Maintain Supply Chain Operations:* Ensure the uninterrupted flow of products and services from suppliers to customers within an acceptable quality level and time frame.
- *Manage Product Development and Manufacturing:* Manage the process of bringing a product from concept to market release.
- *Manage Product Marketing:* Create, produce, and distribute marketing materials.
- *Manage Product Distribution:* Manage logistics of transporting products to customers and distributors.
- *Manage Retailers:* Manage retail functions to sell products to end users.
- *Manage Purchasing:* Manage procurement of raw materials and goods that are necessary for producing products.

Actual supply chains differ greatly depending on the goods involved. Some can be far more vulnerable to climate disruptions than others, based on three main factors: (1) where raw materials and finished products are produced, which depends on labor cost and location of raw materials and factories or processing plants; (2) how goods are moved, which depends not only on their origins and destinations but also on the value, weight, and perishability of products; and (3) the type of destination, which depends on whether goods are for business or household consumption.

---

[1] CISA, "National Critical Functions," 2020, p. 3.

Key assets and geographic distribution all vary with these factors. Depending on the product, raw materials and production could be in the United States or other countries; some materials and production (such as for farming) are highly dispersed, while others (such as for mining of rare earth minerals and production of semiconductors) are fairly concentrated. For goods produced overseas, coastal ports are key assets. According to one study, 99 percent of imports, by weight, travel through ports.[2] In particular, the Port of Los Angeles, the Port of Long Beach, and the Port of New York and New Jersey are the most important for container shipping, with almost half of all containers entering the United States entering via these three ports.[3] The Port of Houston and the Port of South Louisiana are the most-important ports for petrochemicals and bulk goods.[4] Rail and river shipping is important for bulk commodities, such as grains and coal. Most food and manufactured goods, whether imported or domestically produced, move by truck, either for their entire journey or in combination with other modes. Airports handle a small percentage of overall cargo by weight but a disproportionate share of high-value goods (e.g., electronics) and goods that require fast delivery (e.g., perishable foods from overseas, overnight packages).[5] As of 2020, 14 U.S. airports handled mostly cargo.[6] Other key assets, such as factories and warehouses, are much more widely dispersed.

Supply chains include both public- and private-sector actors. Production of most goods is in private hands. Coastal ports, inland ports, and airports are generally owned by public entities, often by special-purpose port authorities, but many private firms work on port property and, in some cases, manage operations.[7] Most carriers (the entities that move goods, regardless of mode) are private, as are the third-party logistics firms that support companies with goods to ship. Trucks and barges are privately owned but depend on public roads and waterways. A further complication is that some of these private entities are highly concentrated (e.g., only seven major railroads serve the entire country), while others are very diffuse (e.g., trucks).

Risk of Disruption Due to Climate Change

A changing climate is expected to lead to an increase in the frequency and severity of extreme weather events, some of which have the potential to disrupt supply chain activities. Tropical cyclones (which include hurricanes) and coastal flooding can damage supply chain assets, such as shipping containers, commercial trucks, and distribution centers; destroy stockpiles

---

[2] Hippe et al., *Estimation of Cost Required to Elevate US Ports in Response to Climate Change.*

[3] U.S. Army Corps of Engineers, "U.S. Waterborne Container Traffic by Port/Waterway in 2020."

[4] Hu et al., *2023 Port Performance Freight Statistics Program.*

[5] International Air Transportation Association, "What Types of Cargo Are Transported by Air?"

[6] Schwieterman and Hague, "The Rise of Cargo-Focused Hub Airports."

[7] Ecola et al., *Rebuilding Surface, Maritime, and Air Transportation in Puerto Rico After Hurricanes Irma and Maria.*

and warehouses; and interrupt freight operations and logistics activities, causing shipping delays and price increases.[8] Hurricanes that are severe enough to disrupt supply chains are projected to become two to four times more frequent by 2040.[9] Similarly, inland flooding can disrupt product distribution by slowing or stopping the movement of products along railways, roads, and rivers,[10] and that disruption contributes to difficulties in managing optimal inventory. In 2020, inland flooding in the Midwest caused supply chain disruptions, interrupting the flow of goods from producers to consumers.[11] Severe storm systems that include heavy snowfall can disrupt production, as well as transportation, if major roads are impassable.[12]

Extreme heat can reduce worker productivity in distribution activities,[13] which can cause shipment delays and potential shortages in some commodities. Additionally, extreme heat can reduce the speed at which products can be moved from producer to consumer and slow the pace of production along different parts of the supply chain.[14] Droughts also disrupt product distribution and can make procuring important production inputs difficult in some regions.[15] Sea-level rise and the resulting extreme tides can lower freight throughput capacity at key logistics hubs in low-lying regions, which could necessitate new supply chain configurations.[16] Transitioning to these new configurations will likely involve a period of increased logistics disruptions and impede inventory management. Finally, wildfires pose

---

[8] Scholz et al., "Impact of Climate Change on Supply Chains"; Smythe, *Assessing the Impacts of Hurricane Sandy on the Port of New York and New Jersey's Maritime Responders and Response Infrastructure*; Sturgis, Smythe, and Tucci, *Port Recovery in the Aftermath of Hurricane Sandy*; U.S. Department of Transportation (DOT), *Supply Chain Assessment of the Transportation Industrial Base*; Van Houtven et al., *Act Now or Pay Later*; Xia and Lindsey, "Port Adaptation to Climate Change and Capacity Investments Under Uncertainty." *Tropical cyclone* is the broadest term and includes tropical depressions, tropical storms, and hurricanes, each of which is characterized by progressively stronger wind speeds.

[9] Scholz et al., "Impact of Climate Change on Supply Chains."

[10] Angel et al., "Midwest"; Pierce, "The Long Haul"; Rossetti, "Potential Impacts of Climate Change on Railroads"; Scholz et al., "Impact of Climate Change on Supply Chains."

[11] Pierce, "The Long Haul."

[12] Mensah et al., "Supply Chain Risks Analysis of a Logging Company."

[13] Zhang and Shindell, "Costs from Labor Losses Due to Extreme Heat in the USA Attributable to Climate Change."

[14] Rossetti, "Potential Impacts of Climate Change on Railroads"; Scholz et al., "Impact of Climate Change on Supply Chains."

[15] Chang, "A Reliable Waterway System Is Important to Agriculture"; Hirtzer, Elkin, and Deaux, "Dwindling Mississippi Grounds Barges, Threatens Shipments"; W. Phillips, "Commodity Shipments Under Threat from Low Mississippi Water Levels"; Scholz et al., "Impact of Climate Change on Supply Chains"; Zamuda et al., *U.S. Energy Sector Vulnerabilities to Climate Change and Extreme Weather*.

[16] AECOM, *Port of Los Angeles*; Allen, McLeod, and Hutt, "Sea Level Rise Exposure Assessment of U.S. East Coast Cargo Container Terminals"; DOT, *Supply Chain Assessment of the Transportation Industrial Base*; Scholz et al., "Impact of Climate Change on Supply Chains"; Slay and Dooley, *Improving Supply Chain Resilience to Manage Climate Change Risks*.

risks to product distribution in the West.[17] Given the importance of the Ports of Los Angeles and Long Beach to regional and national retailers, disruptions from wildfire that delay the distribution of shipments from these ports could cause larger-scale disruptions as wildfires intensify through the end of this century.

Climate change's effects on supply chain assets, logistics, and processes are likely to disrupt the flow of goods between producers and consumers. Disruptions to product distribution can limit retail inventories; cause price spikes for critical inputs; or force product distributors to substitute alternative routes or shipment modes, causing disruptions to day-to-day freight operations and logistics.[18] Additional disruptions due to physical damage to retail facilities and manufacturing plants can also interrupt normal supply chain operations.[19]

Maintain Supply Chains was assessed as facing a risk of moderate disruption from climate change in the baseline period, but that risk was assessed as increasing by 2100 in both current and high emissions scenarios. The baseline risk of moderate disruption is driven by hurricanes, which already affect supply chain assets, activities, and processes. For instance, Hurricanes Katrina and Sandy disrupted normal supply chain processes in multiple states and metropolitan areas.[20] Hurricanes are projected to become severer in the next century.[21] Some of the country's largest ports (the Port of New York and New Jersey and the Port of Savannah for container shipping, and the Port of Houston and the Port of South Louisiana for total tonnage) are on the East Coast or the Gulf Coast, which means that a particularly severe hurricane could pose a risk of major disruption to *Maintain Supply Chains*.

The risk of disruption to *Maintain Supply Chains* is expected to grow through the end of this century for other climate drivers as well. For instance, expected increases in extreme heat, drought, flooding, and sea-level rise currently pose a risk of moderate disruption to *Maintain Supply Chains* but were assessed as posing a risk of major disruption under current emissions by 2100.[22] Under high emissions, the expected increase in floods and extreme heat was assessed as posing a risk of major disruption by 2100.

---

[17] Resilinc, "Wildfires Are Up 30% Year over Year and Wreaking Havoc on Supply Chains."

[18] Chopra and Sodhi, "Reducing the Risk of Supply Chain Disruptions"; Dong et al., *Modeling Multimodal Freight Transportation Network Performance Under Disruptions*; Helper and Soltas, "Why the Pandemic Has Disrupted Supply Chains"; Leibovici and Dunn, "Supply Chain Bottlenecks and Inflation."

[19] Cachon, Gallino, and Olivares, "Severe Weather and Automobile Assembly Productivity."

[20] Skipper, Hanna, and Gibson, "Alabama Power Response to Katrina"; Sturgis, Smythe, and Tucci, *Port Recovery in the Aftermath of Hurricane Sandy*.

[21] Kossin et al., "Extreme Storms."

[22] Easterling et al., "Precipitation Change in the United States"; Mallakpour and Villarini, "The Changing Nature of Flooding Across the Central United States"; Sweet et al., "Sea Level Rise"; Vose et al., "Temperature Changes in the United States."

Subfunction Effects

Maintain Supply Chains has six subfunctions, and five of these face some risk of disruption due to climate change. Climate drivers that strain regional transportation systems can lead to interruptions in the flow of goods between producers and consumers, limited access to critical inputs and resources, and reduced mobility of the supply chain workforce.[23] These disruptions are expected to be larger for *Maintain Supply Chain Operations, Manage Product Development and Manufacturing* (which involves product conceptualization and creation of a minimum viable product), *Manage Product Distribution, Manage Retailers,* and *Manage Purchasing* than for other subfunctions. For subfunctions dedicated to the movement of goods, such as *Maintain Supply Chain Operations,* climate change effects could reach a point at which regional operations fail to meet routine needs. Subfunctions that involve management-related processes are likely to be less affected, although climate change could cause minor issues by the end of the century because of increased logistics costs imposed on managers.

Status of Risk Mitigation

Mitigation of climate risk for *Maintain Supply Chains* is complex, given both the differences among supply chains and the numbers of actors in the private and public sectors. These actors include the following:

- suppliers of raw materials (e.g., farms, ranches, mines)
- producers of finished goods (e.g., processors, factories)
- wholesalers and distributors
- third-party logistics firms
- technology providers that serve shippers and carriers
- utilities that allow businesses to function (e.g., electricity and water providers)
- carriers (e.g., airlines, ocean and river shippers, trucking firms)
- retailers (online and brick and mortar) and institutional customers that procure in bulk (e.g., schools, prisons)
- infrastructure asset owners and operators (e.g., port authorities, state and local departments of transportation, private firms that operate at ports)
- regulators (e.g., government agencies both in the United States and abroad that oversee food and drug safety, customs, and taxes; agencies that require emergency response plans for major assets).

These actors form a complex web of domestic and international business relationships in which each supplier has more than one customer, each producer and wholesaler has multiple suppliers, each third-party logistics firm works with multiple actors, compliance needs differ

---

[23] Scholz et al., "Impact of Climate Change on Supply Chains."

by the type of good and country, large companies operate their own integrated supply chains, major retailers (such as Walmart and Amazon) have sufficient market power to influence their suppliers, and the U.S. government is a major buyer of many goods.

Most *Maintain Supply Chains* mitigation measures commonly used and identified in another Homeland Security Operational Analysis Center report for CISA fall into three categories that address different risks.[24] Each mitigation measure is carried out by a different combination of actors. The three categories are as follows:

- **reducing risk of physical damage to existing infrastructure.** This refers to making physical infrastructure less vulnerable. These strategies address climate drivers that cause physical damage to assets through flooding, severe storm systems, tropical cyclones, and sea-level rise. Measures can include building seawalls, raising docks and wharves, reinforcing dikes, and even physically relocating assets. Changes to major transportation nodes that serve the supply chain would likely be made by asset owners and operators, such as port authorities, likely in conjunction with local, state, or even federal government (depending on the size and cost of the project). For example, deepening a channel at the Port of Savannah (which mitigates the silting that can occur with tropical storms) required 20 years to reach completion, including congressional and mayoral involvement to secure federal funding.[25] Warehouses, manufacturing plants, and vehicle storage facilities would be hardened by each facility's private-sector owner. Relocation could involve a wider group of actors—local governments for land use and permitting, state and federal government for funding—and might also require environmental review, which allows advocacy groups and the public to express their opinions.
- **reducing risk of low inventory.** The risk of low inventory is that insufficient goods would be available to meet demand following a disruption. Low inventory of critical response supplies (e.g., food and water, generators, medical supplies) can greatly affect a disaster response. This mitigation measure encompasses several actions, such as pre-positioning goods to be readily available following a disaster, stockpiling goods that can be easily moved, and incorporating technologies that improve supply chain resilience. Most of these changes would likely be carried out by private-sector actors to reduce their own risk.
- **reducing risk of transportation disruption.** Disruptions could be caused by extreme heat making outdoor work more difficult or by flooding temporarily halting operations. Measures include moving goods via less vulnerable modes and making operational changes to reduce risk. Most of these changes would likely be carried out by private-sector actors to reduce their own risk and might be prompted by regulations. For exam-

---

[24] Lauland et al., *Strategies to Mitigate the Risk to the National Critical Functions Generated by Climate Change.*

[25] Kanell and Bluestein, "Expansion of GA Ports Pays Dividends to Economy, Companies, Jobs."

ple, in spring 2023, Spain announced plans to ban outdoor work during extreme heat.[26] In the railroad industry, it is already established practice to reduce train speeds to reduce the risk of derailment if heat warps rail tracks.[27]

- Drought is a more difficult risk to mitigate. It particularly affects the supply chains for agricultural products (both plants and animals), minerals (mining operations require water), and bulk commodities (which often move by barge on inland waterways). Although bulk commodities could be moved via other modes, the inputs to crops, animals, and mining will be subject to competition for other uses of water (e.g., residential bathing and drinking).

Transformative change for *Maintain Supply Chains* would likely require more federal intervention in industrial policy, such as incentives to reshore manufacturing and spur greater use of three-dimensional (3D) printing to make goods locally. (Although 3D printing still relies on material inputs that might need to be moved from other locations, the ability to print specific products on demand from a printer already in a location would reduce transportation needs.) Automation in supply chains could be transformative in terms of goods movement but costly in the short run, might take a long time to resolve technical challenges, or might be confined to specific goods or geographic areas.

Barriers and Enablers of Risk Mitigation

There are several barriers to pursuing these mitigation strategies:

- As noted above, the very multiplicity of actors and stakeholders across the public and private sectors, both in the United States and abroad, makes implementation of any supply chain–wide mitigation difficult. Major changes require agreement or buy-in from multiple actors, which often have competing interests.
- No one federal agency is responsible for the entire supply chain. DOT regulates and funds various modes of transportation that support the supply chain. U.S. Customs and Border Protection levies tariffs on imported goods. The Transportation Security Administration screens imports that arrive by air to ensure that imported goods do not threaten public safety, while the Maritime Administration (part of DOT) oversees security at seaports. The U.S. Army Corps of Engineers and the U.S. Coast Guard also have regulatory roles for inland waterways and coastal areas.
- Major infrastructure projects involve multiple actors and funding streams, and it can take a long time to reach agreement. For example, the Chicago Region Environmental and Transportation Efficiency (CREATE) Program involves both public and private actors: DOT, the state of Illinois, Cook County, the City of Chicago, Metra (the area's

---

[26] "Spain Plans to Ban Outdoor Work in Extreme Heat."

[27] Austin, "Excessive Heat Can Impact Rails as Well as Driver Health."

commuter rail service), Amtrak, and freight railroads. CREATE started in 2003 and, as of spring 2023, had completed 33 of an anticipated 70 projects.

- Depending on the nature of its business, a private firm might not have the incentives for long-term planning to address climate change. It might also be unwilling to cooperate with other firms for fear of losing a competitive advantage.
- There can be champions and opponents of specific projects among elected officials, various levels of government, and advocacy groups. Because of the length and complexity of projects, these positions can both change over time and necessitate compromises to secure buy-in from all actors.

Two major enablers for some mitigation strategies are that the private sector can likely react more quickly than public agencies can and that private-sector actors might be able to pass costs along to end users (whether business or consumers).

Although the complexity of the supply chain makes it challenging to systematically pursue large-scale climate risk mitigations, as of this writing in October 2023, interest was high in improving supply chain resilience more generally. The coronavirus disease 2019 (COVID-19) pandemic exposed many weaknesses in the supply chain, and measures to increase resilience will likely improve resilience to climate drivers as well. The next section describes some potential measures.

Illustrative Examples of Risk Mitigation Practices

In another report for this project, Lauland et al., *Strategies to Mitigate the Risk to the National Critical Functions Generated by Climate Change*, researchers identified 14 distinct strategies to mitigate climate change's impacts for *Maintain Supply Chains*. We selected four strategies to review in depth here, to cover a variety of strategy types and implementing actors, as well as strategies that mitigate the largest sources of risk for this NCF (flooding and tropical cyclones) and those that the literature shows might be more effective than others:

- strategic stockpiles of critical goods
- port mapping and planning
- blockchain technology to increase supply chain transparency
- land-use planning, zoning, and relocation of critical assets in vulnerable areas.

Strategic Stockpiles of Critical Goods

Stockpiling is holding inventory not for immediate use but as a contingency for future use. Stockpiling can mitigate risk from the four climate drivers that can cause physical damage within *Maintain Supply Chains*: flooding, sea-level rise, severe storm systems, and tropical cyclones. Stockpiled goods, if stored in locations far enough from the site of a natural disaster, can be distributed more quickly than they can through normal supply chains, which could be disrupted by warehouse damage or inaccessible transportation routes.

Both public and private entities can stockpile goods. The federal government maintains a Strategic National Stockpile (SNS) consisting of medical supplies and equipment for use in the event of a large-scale disruption to the medical supply chain. Some of these goods are in 12-hour push packages, meaning that they can be distributed quickly to locations requiring disaster assistance, once requested by a state government. The SNS was most recently tapped in 2017 (following a severe hurricane season) and 2020 (during the COVID-19 pandemic). The Federal Emergency Management Agency (FEMA) also stockpiles food, water, and generators for postdisaster distribution.[28] Through such campaigns as its Ready.gov effort, the federal government can also encourage household stockpiling to reduce demand in the event of a disaster.[29]

Private firms at any point along a supply chain can also stockpile goods to varying degrees. However, stockpiling entails costs, so individual firms must strike a balance between resilience and cost, informed by the likelihood of demand shifts, potential transportation bottlenecks, and storage costs. Depending on the good, stockpiling can also affect prices across the supply chain. For example, when suppliers stockpiled a rare earth element because of rising prices, the market responded with an even larger price increase.[30]

Implementation Issues

Depending on the circumstances, stockpiling can be effective and feasible. At a posthurricane roundtable to better understand supply chain resilience, one beverage company noted that it continued to keep high inventory in certain hurricane-prone regions because demand often remains high when storms are likely.[31] Feasibility in particular depends on the nature of the commodity. The cost of the goods and storage capacity requirements are factors that make stockpiling more suited to some commodities than to others. Perishable goods are difficult to stockpile without an effective policy to move goods that are nearing their expiration date to consumers (a policy called *sell-one-stock-one*[32]). Stockpile maintenance needs also differ by the type of good, with perishable items, such as food and medication, needing to be replenished based on expiration dates. Even goods that are not perishable in the short term (e.g., batteries, lightbulbs, textiles) can degrade over time and need to be replaced.

---

[28] Siripurapu and Berman, "The State of U.S. Strategic Stockpiles."

[29] U.S. Department of Homeland Security, "Ready."

[30] Sprecher et al., "Framework for Resilience in Material Supply Chains, with a Case Study from the 2010 Rare Earth Crisis."

[31] Meyer and Meyer, "Supply Chain Resilience."

[32] Liu, Song, and Tong, "Building Supply Chain Resilience Through Virtual Stockpile Pooling."

Stockpiling is a routine issue for both public and private entities that are involved with the supply chain. However, there are recurring barriers, especially for the following:

- **consumer panic buying.** Some literature notes that households tend to purchase more than they require when storms are predicted. This reality can make it challenging to stockpile the appropriate amount of inventory. This is especially true of certain goods, such as bottled water, that are in high demand following hurricanes.[33]

- **visibility into supply chains, especially in emergencies.** If communication channels are disrupted, it can be difficult for both public- and private-sector actors, along with the public, to know which goods are being delivered where. One example is that, following Hurricane Sandy, many gas stations were closed and drivers were unable to find reliable information about which gas stations were open and how much gasoline they had.[34]

- **amount of stockpiling needed.** Different commodities might be needed in different volumes depending on the scale of the natural disaster. Although this issue is not specific to climate change, the SNS was unable to supply sufficient personal protective equipment (PPE) during the first part of the COVID-19 pandemic, and many health care workers and entities had to source their own or use PPE past its usual life. The SNS had not stocked enough PPE for a national pandemic.[35]

- **government support of the supply chain.** Most critical goods are manufactured by the private sector, and private entities have an incentive to maintain sufficient stockpiles based on their own business planning. However, these stockpiles might not meet demand for critical goods in emergencies, or they might not be able to be delivered in a timely fashion. In this case, these goods would need to be part of government stockpiles, such as the SNS or FEMA's stockpiles.[36]

- **delays in shipping stockpiled goods.** As one report notes, there are three sources of potential delay in distributing goods from the SNS: delays in state requests for assistance, in disaster declarations, and in shipping.[37] A report by the U.S. Department of Homeland Security's Office of Inspector General notes that, following Hurricane Maria, FEMA lost track of nearly 40 percent of "life-sustaining commodity shipments" to Puerto Rico and that the shipments that were delivered took, on average, 69 days to reach their destinations.[38]

---

[33] Pan et al., "Pre-Hurricane Consumer Stockpiling and Post-Hurricane Product Availability."

[34] Meyer and Meyer, "Supply Chain Resilience."

[35] Mehrotra, Malani, and Yadav, "Personal Protective Equipment Shortages During COVID-19."

[36] Ergun, Hopp, and Keskinocak, "A Structured Overview of Insights and Opportunities for Enhancing Supply Chain Resilience."

[37] Paul and Hariharan, "Location-Allocation Planning of Stockpiles for Effective Disaster Mitigation."

[38] Office of Inspector General, *FEMA Mismanaged the Commodity Distribution Process in Response to Hurricanes Irma and Maria.*

Some enablers have been proposed recently:

- **virtual stockpile pooling.** This is the practice of holding physical stockpiles in multiple locations while managing the total amount across all locations. For example, Johnson and Johnson uses this technique to ensure that it always has sufficient stockpiles to meet the requirements of its contract with the federal government for specific quantities to be supplied in case of an emergency.[39]
- **common stockpiling.** This is the practice of multiple actors maintaining common inventory that can be accessed by multiple entities during an emergency. However, this involves its own complexities:

  > forecasting joint disruption likelihoods across different groups of end users, design of the stockpiling network taking into account security, cost, and lead time of storage and transportation options, [and] design of operational strategies such as when and to whom to release stockpile inventory.[40]

As climate impacts increase, stockpiling strategies can adapt. A future with more climate-induced disruptions could have an increased need for stockpiling and prepositioning supplies needed for emergency response, in increased quantities, in new types of goods that are not currently stockpiled, or in more areas of the country. The SNS or FEMA program could expand to meet these needs. Or retailers could, either of their own volition or in response to government orders, severely restrict purchases of certain items to decrease panic buying.[41]

Port Mapping and Planning

We define *port mapping and planning* as modeling the potential climate disruptions that could affect specific locations within a specific seaport and adjusting port plans and operations to increase resilience. This can mitigate risk by identifying the most-vulnerable assets based on specific climate drivers and taking actions to reduce the risk. This strategy can mitigate risk from all climate drivers that affect *Maintain Supply Chains*: flooding, sea-level rise, severe storm systems, tropical cyclones, drought, wildfires, and extreme heat.[42] The strategy can both prevent physical damage to the buildings and infrastructure in areas vulnerable to

---

[39] Liu, Song, and Tong, "Building Supply Chain Resilience Through Virtual Stockpile Pooling."

[40] Ergun, Hopp, and Keskinocak, "A Structured Overview of Insights and Opportunities for Enhancing Supply Chain Resilience," p. 64.

[41] For additional information on stockpiling, see Siripurapu and Berman, "The State of U.S. Strategic Stockpiles," or Kulken and Gottron, "The Strategic National Stockpile."

[42] The only driver that affects *Maintain Supply Chains* that is not included here is extreme cold. Our previous risk assessment work showed that this would not cause disruption to the *Maintain Supply Chains* NCF because extreme cold is projected to decrease. Although extreme cold can affect the supply chain, the level of disruption overall is expected to be low. See Miro et al., *Assessing Risk to National Critical Functions as a Result of Climate Change.*

those climate drivers and suggest operational improvements that could mitigate the impacts of drought and extreme heat.

This type of planning would be carried out by the port owner. This could involve a mix of public- and private-sector entities, depending on the governance structure at an individual port. Most U.S. ports are publicly owned by a local government, state government, or port authority. Ports are generally organized into one of two broad models: the landlord model, in which the public owner serves as a landlord and operations are carried out by the port's tenants, or the public service port model, in which the public owner also operates the port.[43] In both cases, the planning would be led by the public owner, but planning done by a port in a landlord model might involve significant input from private-sector tenants. Tenants would develop and carry out their own plans; for example, a tenant at the Port of New York and New Jersey purchased new cranes with elevated motors after previous crane motors were flooded and thus unusable following Hurricane Sandy.[44]

This strategy is aimed primarily at seaports, although some large airports sited in coastal areas of the United States also are vulnerable to sea-level rise and flooding. Although airports can conduct similar mapping and planning, the need is greater for seaports because, by definition, they are on bodies of water and are more vulnerable overall to sea-level rise and flooding. This strategy could have some indirect impacts on other transportation modes that serve ports (road and rail), as well as on warehousing that occurs at or near ports.

Implementation Issues

Although this strategy is highly feasible, it is not necessarily effective as a stand-alone strategy. It is feasible because ports already do extensive planning, and some have already begun developing climate-specific plans. For example, the Port of Long Beach in southern California, one of the country's busiest ports for container shipping, published its *Climate Adaptation and Coastal Resiliency Plan* in 2016. This plan was based on extensive inundation maps developed for potentially 3 inches of sea-level rise, as well as two tide conditions: daily high tide and extreme tides (the 1-percent annual chance of still-water elevation). Based on these inundation maps, the plan defines which piers, roads, rail tracks, buildings, utilities, and breakwaters are at risk under which conditions. The plan then develops specific mitigations in terms of governance, initiatives (continuing evaluations), and infrastructure. As part of a mitigation strategy to address climate change impacts through port policies, plans, and guidelines, the plan provides climate-specific language to be incorporated into eight existing planning documents.[45]

---

[43] Ecola et al., *Rebuilding Surface, Maritime, and Air Transportation in Puerto Rico After Hurricanes Irma and Maria.*

[44] Leonard, "As Storms Become More Frequent and Volatile, Some Ports Plan for the Risk—but Most Do Not."

[45] Port of Long Beach, *Climate Adaptation and Coastal Resiliency Plan (CRP).*

This measure is not effective on its own because climate plans, in and of themselves, do not achieve their goals; they must be implemented on an ongoing basis. Also, planning for climate change can become siloed unless there is an effort to ensure that the plan recommendations are propagated throughout a port's operations and infrastructure planning.

The planning process itself does not engender maintenance requirements. For specific actions, maintenance requirements developed as part of a master plan would vary from port to port, depending on the specifics of each port. Port planning is already mature as an activity, although some ports probably have a greater capacity for long-term planning than others have.

One enabler could be funding incentives at the state level. For example, Florida requires that each port update its master plan every five years to qualify for funding through the Florida Seaport Transportation and Economic Development Program.[46] A report prepared for Texas ports encouraged the Texas Department of Transportation to provide additional funding to support projects to improve resilience.[47]

In terms of barriers, effective planning can be hindered by modeling that does not incorporate up-to-date climate parameters, such as expected sea-level rise or storm surge; a lack of senior leadership to champion climate planning; and a failure to incorporate plan recommendations into decisions about infrastructure and operations. A few port resilience planning guides already exist, such as American Association of Port Authorities, "Port Planning and Investment Toolkit"; Morris and Sempier, *A Port Management Self-Assessment*; and U.S. Climate Resilience Toolkit, "Ports Resilience Index."

Blockchain Technology to Increase Supply Chain Transparency

Blockchain is a technology that allows users to create a decentralized set of transaction data. A block is a data structure that captures new information, and a chain is the thing that links them together. The information that individual users enter into the blockchain is distributed among all users, making it very difficult to change any of the information within the blockchain. Although best known for its role in facilitating cryptocurrency, a blockchain can be used for any set of data.

Incorporating blockchain into a supply chain reduces risk because it provides a set of data about all links within a supply chain that any of the users can access. This visibility mitigates risk indirectly because, although it would not prevent goods from being damaged or destroyed, it allows users to gain information quickly about the location of goods, as well as where they have been and where they are being shipped. This would address climate risk from all climate drivers that affect *Maintain Supply Chains*: flooding, sea-level rise, severe storm systems, tropical cyclones, drought, wildfire, and extreme heat.[48] The strategy can

---

[46] Littlejohn, Mann and Associates, *Seaports Resiliency Report*.

[47] Bathgate et al., *Creating a Resilient Port System in Texas*.

[48] We excluded extreme cold because it is expected to decrease.

reduce the potential for resource constraints because many other NCFs rely on supply chains, and it can also address demand change, especially when demand for specific goods shifts based on climate drivers (for example, drought could increase demand for agricultural inputs in some regions and decrease it in others because the ability to grow certain crops in certain locations could change over time).

This mitigation would be implemented by private-sector actors all along the supply chain: suppliers, processors, manufacturers, wholesalers, distributors, and retailers. For blockchain to have its fullest impact, it would need to be adopted throughout a supply chain, not by only one actor.

Implementation Issues

Given the right circumstances, blockchain could be effective in improving supply chain visibility and reducing costs and delays, all of which could mitigate climate risks, at least indirectly. However, feasibility is more challenging because, to be effective, multiple actors in a particular supply chain must cooperate. One article, tellingly titled "Blockchain's Disconnect Between the Could-Be and the Has-Been," notes,

> Businesses understand the inherent advantage blockchain would bring to key functions, ensuring greater visibility, higher capacity utilization, and possibly helping to drive down costs across the system. But yet, blockchain does not seem to inch past highly advertised pilot programs happening across in [sic] the supply chain ecosystem.[49]

In one example, a blockchain platform called TradeLens, which was set up jointly between an ocean shipping line (Maersk) and a technology company (IBM), closed within four years, ending operations in early 2023. The reasons cited were a lack of customers, particularly among Asian shippers (who play a major role in ocean shipping); the emergence of a competing blockchain platform; the challenge of creating digital documents that can be accepted across multiple jurisdictions, and the fact that Maersk is itself a major shipper and might not have been seen as a neutral party.[50]

Although there are some commercial platforms on the market, the technology continues to evolve and is not yet considered mature. There are varying predictions of when it might be more widely adopted. A 2020 article on the food supply chain suggested that mainstream adoption was five to ten years away.[51] In a 2022 survey, 68 percent of respondents said that they thought they would be using blockchain in five years.[52] A 2023 article focusing on the

---

[49] "Blockchain's Disconnect Between the Could-Be and the Has-Been."

[50] Mearian, "Maersk's TradeLens Demise Likely a Death Knell for Blockchain Consortiums."

[51] Murphy, "Who Is Buying into IBM's Blockchain Dreams?"

[52] Magill and Lopez, "The Top Technologies Creating a 'Revolutionary Stage' in Supply Chains."

construction industry noted that using blockchain to track and predict material flow was still several years away.[53]

Sharkey, "Q&A," cites three main barriers to implementing blockchain in a supply chain:

- **lack of trust between members of a supply chain.** Although, in theory, blockchain should engender higher trust than a system without it does because it creates a set of data that is very difficult for users to change, in practice, there is a lack of trust between supply chain actors. One article noted that "data-sharing [has been] looked upon as market suicide in certain aspects."[54] Blockchain would need to overcome this initial trust barrier.
- **lack of industry consensus on the best approach.** In addition to the multiplicity of supply chain actors, which might have different market strategies and competing interests, many goods are shipped internationally, and documentation needs to comply with multiple regulations.
- **complexity and nontransparency of the technology.** A survey taken in 2022 asked private-sector supply chain actors which of 11 technologies they had adopted. Only 10 percent said that they were using blockchain, the lowest among the 11 technologies, and 20 percent of surveyed firms said that they did not understand the "technological landscape," the highest such score among the 11 technologies.[55]

One enabler could be specific business cases for blockchain; it might be too expensive and complex for all supply chains. A 2022 article quoted a supply chain consultant: "Blockchain has the potential to make significant improvements in security, transparency, and governance, but only in supply chains where there is value in controlling consumer risk, valuable goods or complying with regulations."[56] Other enablers would be (1) ease of use of specific platforms and (2) companies being more familiar with the advantages and disadvantages of the technology platforms. It might also be helpful for trusted trade associations to take an active role to encourage adoption. For example, the Digital Container Shipping Association, a trade association of container-shipping firms, is developing standards to accelerate digitization of the supply chain.[57]

In addition to the visibility of goods within the supply chain, some supply chains would see cobenefits. Many early adopters were part of food supply chains, both for tracing outbreaks of foodborne illness and for tracking the provenance of ingredients. In 2018, Walmart mandated that its leafy-green suppliers adopt blockchain so that it could better track the source

---

[53] Lawrence, "How Contractors Use Tech to Tighten Up Supply Chains."

[54] "Blockchain's Disconnect Between the Could-Be and the Has-Been."

[55] Magill and Lopez, "The Top Technologies Creating a 'Revolutionary Stage' in Supply Chains."

[56] Lockridge, "Blockchain, Once Overhyped, Is Finding Real Transportation Use Cases."

[57] Digital Container Shipping Association, homepage.

of an outbreak if greens were found to be contaminated. Blockchain enables a process to be completed in seconds that previously took days.[58] An environmental nonprofit worked with a technology firm to develop a blockchain system that allowed consumers to confirm where their fish were caught.[59] IBM introduced a platform called Food Trust to provide blockchain on a subscription basis for actors all along the food supply chain, but critics have noted that there are few incentives for suppliers to provide information, and several firms that tested Food Trust have since stopped using it.[60]

Land-Use Planning, Zoning, and Relocation of Critical Assets in Vulnerable Areas

Although land use, zoning, and asset relocation are three distinct issues, they share a goal of ensuring that infrastructure is less exposed to disruption from climate drivers. This strategy can mitigate risk from flooding, sea-level rise, severe storm systems, and tropical cyclones by preventing physical damage to the buildings and infrastructure in areas vulnerable to these climate drivers.

Land-use planning is the process of assigning a certain type of land use (e.g., residential, commercial, light industrial) to areas within a jurisdiction. Land-use planning is generally conducted at the local level by either municipal or county governments, depending on the nature of local jurisdictions. Land-use plans can cover entire jurisdictions or specific neighborhoods.

The process of writing a land-use plan can be political and sometimes contentious, depending on the involvement of local stakeholders—developers, major institutions, environmental and business advocacy groups, and the public—whose interests can clash. Stakeholders often press for land-use changes they see as desirable, such as opening vacant land for development, preserving land as open space, and converting land from one use to another (such as reclaiming formerly industrial land for housing or open space).

Adopting a new land-use plan does not necessarily change existing land uses in the short term, for a variety of reasons. Land might be specified in a plan for one type of use, but another use might exist if a building or structure had been exempted. Or land might be vacant, even if building is allowed, because developers have not built there. Finally, land-use changes can take years, even decades, to occur because developers' willingness to build in certain areas is affected by many factors (e.g., demand for specific uses, costs of land and construction, need for remediation, the presence and capacity of utilities and other infrastructure). Land can be developed either by a private developer or company or by an entity in the public sector (for example, most airports in the United States are owned by public-sector entities).

---

[58] Smith, "In Wake of Romaine E. coli Scare, Walmart Deploys Blockchain to Track Leafy Greens"; Wells, "Walmart Mandates Blockchain Use for Leafy Greens Suppliers."

[59] Kincaid, "Is Grocery Store Salmon Really Wild?"

[60] Murphy, "Who Is Buying into IBM's Blockchain Dreams?"

Zoning is how land-use plans are implemented. Zoning is usually more specific in terms of building types allowed on specific land parcels (e.g., not simply single-family residential but also allowable lot size and building footprint). Local governments with zoning authority typically have zoning maps designating these uses and zoning boards that decide whether land uses proposed by private or public entities conform to these uses. Both land-use planning and zoning can mitigate risk by disallowing certain uses in vulnerable areas (for example, prohibiting construction in flood-prone areas) and steering development to less risky areas.

Asset relocation refers to building new physical supply chain assets (e.g., factories, warehouses, ports) in less vulnerable areas. Generally, the owners of the asset (whether in the private or public sector) obtain approval for and then build a new asset to an area zoned for that type of land use. This can mitigate risk by moving important supply chain assets out of vulnerable locations. Nike, which produces clothing and shoes, has moved several facilities in Southeast Asia out of floodplains.[61]

Several resources are available to help with land-use planning for climate resilience:

- Georgetown Climate Center, "Managed Retreat Toolkit"
- Office of Planning Advocacy, "Municipal Climate Resilience Planning Guide"
- U.S. Climate Resilience Toolkit, "Planning and Land Use"
- U.S. Environmental Protection Agency, "Brownfields Road Map"
- U.S. Environmental Protection Agency, "Flood Resilience Checklist"

Implementation Issues

The effectiveness of this strategy could be very high in specific locations, for specific elements in the supply chain, depending on the type of buildings and infrastructure threatened by climate drivers. The strategy would be less effective if risks spread to locations that were not previously at risk (e.g., if an area that did not previously experience sunny-day flooding began to experience it).

However, this strategy is likely feasible only in certain conditions and for certain types of buildings and infrastructure. Two main factors are

- how easily an asset, or the functions that it houses, can be built in a new location. A coastal seaport needs to be on the water on a coast, and extraction of raw materials needs to take place where those materials are located. However, warehousing functions can be moved from one building to another.
- whether sufficient buildable land exists in appropriate locations. Airports require a substantial amount of land, and the largest are in metropolitan areas, where developable land is usually limited. Other functions, such as factories and warehouses, need to be

---

[61] Xie, "Nike."

near roads or rail and near population centers for access to both the workforce and the markets they serve.

Maintenance requirements are not a major factor because similar assets would entail similar maintenance, and perhaps even less, if they were simply located elsewhere. Local governments already have and exercise land-use planning and zoning authority.

This strategy faces more barriers than enablers. Barriers include the following:

- **Land-use plans and zoning codes might not take climate threats into account.** Because they can be complex and difficult to change, in many locations, land-use plans and zoning codes were adopted in an era when climate change was not considered a major threat. For example, even if a private company wanted to build a new factory because a current location was threatened by frequent flooding, the existing zoning code might still have that area labeled as appropriate for industrial uses, and land in less threatened areas might not be zoned for industrial use.
- **Land-use plans and zoning codes could encounter opposition.** Land-use plans and zoning codes can engender controversy when attempts are made to update them (for example, from neighborhood residents opposing land uses that they consider incompatible [i.e., they cannot coexist because one use inhibits the other] or that create negative externalities, such as heavy truck traffic). Even if a land-use plan or zoning code allows the types of industrial uses that are required for supply chains, community or political opposition can lengthen or shut down the process of receiving approval to relocate buildings or structures or build new ones.
- **Zoning approval processes can be lengthy.** Zoning codes can be *by right*, which means that specific approval is not required if the proposed development meets the code specifications. But most zoning codes require approvals for individual projects, meaning that the zoning board can require changes to a development plan before approving it. Even if the changes ultimately result in approval, the process can be lengthy, result in substantial changes, and add substantial costs.
- **The permitting process can be lengthy.** If development might harm environmental resources, it is typically subject to environmental review and approval before permits to build can be issued. Depending on the nature of the proposed building or structure, permits might be required from state or federal agencies (such as departments of environmental protection, air and water quality, and wildlife protection). The environmental studies required for major projects can take years to complete (a 2020 study found an average of 4.5 years across all federal agencies).
- **The costs of moving infrastructure and (when necessary) demolishing or remediating unused infrastructure can be high.** The types of supply chain infrastructure that need to be relocated can be prohibitively expensive to move. Some buildings, such as warehouses, might not be costly to relocate, but factories with specialized equipment or railyards might fall into this category. In addition, some types of infrastructure might

incur the expense of being demolished (if the land is being reverted to another use, such as open space) or remediated (if potentially harmful pollutants are present). Remediation costs are generally folded into the overall cost of site redevelopment.

- **For large projects, competing interests of multiple actors can make it difficult to reach agreement.** The supply chain is a complex web of public and private actors. Although most goods are produced, moved, and distributed by private companies, these companies move goods on public infrastructure and require public approvals to build factories and warehouses. Public and private entities might interact in other ways, such as local or state governments providing public incentives to locate businesses in their jurisdictions for economic development reasons. Elected officials can also champion or oppose specific projects. For example, the then-mayor of Denver had run for office in 1983 on a platform of building a new airport; after the city negotiated with other local jurisdictions and the two largest airlines, the new airport opened in 1995. This example illustrates not only that having a political champion is important but that, even with a champion, major projects require buy-in from other stakeholders and can take decades to complete.
- **Finally, community members might support or oppose development that enables supply chain operations, and they can express their views in the environmental review or vote for representatives who promise to promote or cancel specific projects.** For example, Amazon's plan to build part of its second headquarters in New York was cancelled because of public opposition.

This strategy could be enabled by

- adopting land-use plans and zoning codes that accurately reflect climate risk and that allow the location or relocation of buildings and structures that support the supply chain (e.g., in 2021, Boston adopted a new Coastal Flood Resilience Overlay District, which restricts development in certain flood-prone areas)
- providing financial incentives to relocate critical infrastructure that would seriously disrupt other functions if damaged or destroyed by a natural disaster
- revising the federal role in permitting to allow projects to move forward more quickly (at the federal level, a Federal Permitting Improvement Steering Council reduces permitting timelines for specific projects)
- using eminent domain to acquire land for relocating assets at risk. However, this can be controversial because it almost inevitably creates winners and losers.

Summary

As noted earlier, the major supply chain disruptions caused by COVID-19 were widespread and encouraged the many actors in supply chains to focus on resilience. One positive outcome from this experience was renewed public attention to supply chains, which do not generally garner much attention unless disruptions are widespread. So, this might be a good moment to consider measures that increase resilience across all types of supply chains, and many private firms and asset owners are doing just that. On the other hand, major hardening and potential relocation of key supply chain assets will require buy-in from numerous actors and stakeholders and might be more difficult to achieve.

Table 2.1 summarizes the four mitigation strategies. Their overall feasibility is most directly affected by economic, technological, and institutional factors. For economic factors, some of these strategies involve private-sector actors, which are unlikely to undertake actions that might have a negative impact on their profitability or might benefit competitors. These strategies could be more feasible in some business cases than in others; they could also be helped by regulations or incentive programs. On the public side, actions that would be undertaken by owners are likely more feasible for large and better-resourced actors or those that are able to successfully garner funding from multiple sources. Technological feasibility is more important for the blockchain strategy. Although commercially available, blockchain remains an emerging technology with which many private firms are not entirely comfortable, and the industry is only starting to work on platforms that might provide standardization. Finally, all strategies are affected by institutional factors because every supply chain for a different type of goods involves a specific mix of private, federal, and SLTT actors. Feasibility depends in many cases on these actors' ability to work together.

TABLE 2.1

Summary of Climate Risk Mitigation Strategies for *Maintain Supply Chains*

Risk Mitigation Strategy	Enabler	Barrier
Strategically stockpiling critical goods is creating inventories of products that are meant to serve as a contingency for future use. This mitigates risk by having goods stored in multiple locations or in locations away from potential damage from climate change drivers. This strategy can be implemented by private companies or governments.	Stockpiling can be enabled by virtual stockpiling (meaning that one stockpile is managed across multiple locations) or common stockpiling (meaning that multiple actors can draw from a single stockpile).	Barriers to effective stockpiling include consumer panic buying (which makes it hard to predict needs), lack of visibility, balancing the needed amounts with the cost of maintaining stockpiles, market failure when private firms' stockpiles would not meet needs, and delays in shipping stockpiled goods.
Port mapping and planning is modeling potential disruptions from climate drivers at individual ports and considering how to prevent or alleviate disruptions in advance. This mitigates physical damage to port infrastructure. Mapping and planning would be carried out by port owners and operators, which can mean a mix of public and private actors, depending on the ports' governance structure.	Some ports already do such mapping and planning. More ports might be encouraged to do so through incentive programs.	Although there are no major barriers to conducting mapping and planning, mapping and planning are much more effective if they incorporate the most-recent climate data available for a specific location. Other barriers to success include a lack of leadership and a failure to incorporate plan results into operations and infrastructure planning.
Using blockchain technology to increase supply chain transparency is incorporating blockchain into supply chain transactions. Blockchain is a technology that allows users to create a decentralized set of transaction data. These hard-to-change data could mitigate some risks from most climate drivers because they would allow greater visibility into the location of goods along the supply chain. This strategy would be implemented by private companies.	Blockchain has been adopted more readily in specific use cases in which transparency and provenance information are required by regulation (such as food supply chains).	One major barrier is the need for all actors along a specific supply chain to use the same technology platform. If they do not, the effectiveness of the strategy decreases. Other barriers include a lack of trust between firms in a specific supply chain, which can limit their desire to share information; a lack of industry standards; and poor understanding of how the technology works.
Land-use planning, zoning, and relocation of critical assets in vulnerable areas are mechanisms to relocate supply chain infrastructure that is vulnerable to climate drivers that can damage physical assets. Land-use planning and zoning are local government functions, and decisions about relocating assets would likely be led by owners, whether private or public, and involve numerous other actors.	This strategy is likelier to work for some types of supply chain assets (such as warehouses) than for others (airports). Other enablers include land-use plans and zoning codes that incorporate climate drivers and the availability of suitable land.	Barriers can include lack of appropriate land for relocation, zoning that does not support desired locations, land-use and zoning plans that do not take climate into account, political and community opposition, and lengthy review processes.

CHAPTER 3

Provide Insurance Services

National Critical Function Overview and Risk Due to Climate Change

Description of the National Critical Function

Insurance is an agreement that facilitates the transfer of risk between members of society. Generally, insurance provides a mechanism for a group to pool funds to pay for losses realized by its individual members. As a function, *Provide Insurance Services* encompasses the delivery of the full spectrum of insurance products, including traditional insurance contracts (e.g., property insurance, commercial general liability insurance), various surety services (e.g., performance bonds), and over-the-counter derivatives (e.g., interest rate swaps). To generate these products, the function also includes processes, such as underwriting, claims payment, pricing, the fulfillment of legal requirements, and providing certainty of payment on losses. CISA breaks this NCF into three subfunctions:

- *Provide Surety Services*
- *Negotiate Over-the-Counter Derivatives to Transfer Risk*
- *Pool Multiple Exposures to Transfer Insurable Risk.*

The primary stakeholders for this function are insurers and reinsurers of all types and sizes, policyholders, and state and federal regulators. This function is geographically decentralized, with assets and operations dispersed widely throughout the country.

Risk of Disruption Due to Climate Change

Climate change is likelier to have impacts on property insurance than on other lines. As flooding, sea-level rise, and wildfire increase with climate change, property insurers will be exposed to greater losses.[1] Absent interventions, these losses could result in insolvencies and adaptation as communities build back in ways that mitigate future risk.[2] At the same time,

---

[1] Bevere and Weigel, "Natural Catastrophes in 2020."

[2] Kunreuther, Michel-Kerjan, and Ranger, "Insuring Future Climate Catastrophes."

residents in these areas will demand more insurance because they face greater risks.[3] Yet, because insurance pricing depends on historical data generated by stable underlying processes, experts expect climate change to challenge underwriters and increase uncertainty and variability in risk estimates.[4] This uncertainty could result in higher costs for residents, which could affect insurance affordability and the ability to buy down risk through residential adaptation. Furthermore, because climate drivers tend to affect whole regions, opportunities for risk transfer are likely to decline in regions that have worse climate impacts.[5]

These pressures on the property insurance market will likely have several impacts on this NCF. Insurers will likely raise premiums and narrow or deny coverage in areas facing higher or more-variable risk due to climate change.[6] As a result, absent market interventions in affected areas, homeowners are likelier to be underinsured or uninsured entirely.[7] This scenario is already beginning to play out in rural California counties facing increased wildfire risk. In 2019, the California Department of Insurance intervened to impose a one-year moratorium on nonrenewals for property insurance in wildfire-prone areas.[8] Dixon, Tsang, and Fitts showed that premiums increased faster in high-risk wildfire areas than elsewhere in the state, leading homeowners to choose higher deductibles and lower coverage limits relative to value and increasing the share of homeowners seeking coverage through the state's high-risk pool, the California Fair Access to Insurance Requirements (FAIR) Plan.[9]

Although insurance markets are generally functioning at present, this NCF was assessed as being at risk of minimal disruption in the baseline scenario because of climate change's current impacts on wildfire risk and property insurance in California. As the climate drivers sea-level rise, flooding, and tropical cyclone (which includes hurricanes) increase, disruptions to this market are expected to rise but remain assessed as being at risk of minimal disruption by 2050 under the current emissions scenario. In a recent analysis, for example, Swiss Re forecasted growth to property insurance markets and premiums but no major disruptions.[10] Given the elevated risk of flooding in 2050 under the high emissions scenario, we surmised that regional impacts to this NCF are likelier than local ones. We therefore assessed it to be at risk of moderate disruption in this scenario by the middle of the 21st century. In both scenarios, climate drivers have the potential to produce problematic correlated losses

---

[3]   K. Baker, "Climate Change Will Offer Long-Term Tailwinds."

[4]   Kunreuther and Michel-Kerjan, *Climate Change, Insurability of Large-Scale Disasters and the Emerging Liability Challenge.*

[5]   Grimaldi et al., "Climate Change and P&C Insurance."

[6]   Fagan, Preudhomme, and Demir, *Insurance Costs Trends Becoming a Headache for the CRE Market.*

[7]   Ramnath and Jeziorski, "Homeowners Insurance and Climate Change."

[8]   California Department of Insurance, "Mandatory One Year Moratorium on Non-Renewals."

[9]   Dixon, Tsang, and Fitts, "California Wildfires."

[10]   Swiss Re, "In a World of Growing Risk the Insurance Industry Has a Crucial Role to Play."

regionally through flooding, sea-level rise, tropical cyclones, and wildfire by the end of the century; we therefore assessed it as being at risk of moderate disruption by 2100.

Status of Risk Mitigation

The Lauland et al. report on mitigation strategies for climate change offers several unique strategies for *Provide Insurance Services*:[11]

- Implement community wildfire protection planning.
- Harden buildings and infrastructure against fire.
- Improve and measure ecological forest management.
- Improve estimates of risk of flooding (e.g., the National Flood Insurance Program's Risk Rating 2.0 pricing approach).
- Improve estimates of risk of wildfire.
- Provide government reinsurance for catastrophic events.
- Strengthen building codes and standards.

In the following discussion, we categorize these strategies as those that reduce vulnerabilities or those that mitigate consequences depending on whether they focus on addressing physical impacts or adapting insurance markets to increasing risks.

Strategies to Reduce Vulnerabilities

Policyholders and their communities can directly reduce their exposure to the physical impacts of natural hazards driven by climate change. This set of strategies is not specific to this NCF: Increased threats to infrastructure and property generally are central to climate change risk. Thus, **adaptations that increase the resilience of property or infrastructure to climate change** support *Provide Insurance Services*. Policyholders could consider such measures as individuals or through their state and local governments. The insurance industry provides some support for such adaptations through certain organizations, such as the Insurance Institute for Business and Home Safety (IBHS), which lists several insurers and states where premium credits or other incentives are offered to insured entities that comply with various resilience criteria.[12] The basic idea behind these adaptations is to increase the information available, harden property against natural hazards through infrastructure or building-specific changes, or relocate buildings and activities away from threats. Although

---

[11] Lauland et al., *Strategies to Mitigate the Risk to the National Critical Functions Generated by Climate Change*.

[12] IBHS, "Financial Incentives."

such adaptations are discussed widely elsewhere, we include examples of some of the measures available, by hazard of concern, in Table 3.1.[13]

TABLE 3.1

Illustrative Adaptation Strategies to Reduce Risks of Climate Change to Property

Adaptation Type	Adaptation Strategy, by Natural Hazard		
	Flooding	Sea-Level Rise	Wildfire
Infrastructure	Construct new infrastructure (e.g., levees).	Construct new infrastructure (e.g., seawalls).	
	Apply green infrastructure strategies.	Maintain and restore wetlands.	
	Repair and retrofit facilities.	Repair and retrofit facilities.	
Land use	Preserve coastal land and development.	Preserve coastal land and development.	Modify land use, reducing construction at the urban–wildlife interface.
	Modify land use to reduce development in floodplains.	Modify land use to reduce development of coastal areas.	Monitor vegetation changes in watersheds.
	Maintain and restore wetlands.	Improve shoreline maintenance using hard strategies (such as seawalls, bulkheads, or revêtements) or soft strategies (such as marshes, dunes, or revised zoning to prohibit shoreline development).	Use controlled burns, thinning, and weed and invasive plant control to reduce risk in wildfire-prone areas.
		Preserve habitat.	
Planning and monitoring	Consider stormwater management logistics.	Monitor sea-level rise and improve models to understand its impacts.	Analyze current fire management capabilities and monitoring efforts, model expected conditions, and anticipate potential future fire events.
	Monitor precipitation and sea-level rise, and improve models to understand their impacts on future flood conditions.		Practice and regularly update management plans to reduce fire risk.
	Provide public awareness and coordination.	Provide public awareness and coordination.	Provide public awareness and coordination.

---

[13] Environmental Resilience Institute, "Strategies for Climate Change Adaptation."

Strategies to Mitigate Consequences

More specific to this function is that insurers and reinsurers, as well as state and federal regulators, can act to buttress insurance markets and work together to harness the capability of insurance premiums to communicate information about risk. Critically, these actions can and should take place in harmony with individual and community actions to mitigate climate change risk. In brief, insurers and reinsurers can **increase capital reserves for property insurance, use underwriting and pricing to incentivize risk reduction generally and climate change adaptation specifically,** and **create new insurance products** (e.g., parametric policies, such as catastrophe bonds, addressed in Table 3.1) **to underwrite hazards at extreme levels.** Information that state and local governments provide to insurers about climate change adaptations can support this process. For example, insurers could advise whether they view different adaptation options as credible and could estimate percentage changes in property insurance rates for them. In this vein, Swiss Re noted that "[i]nvesting in sustainable infrastructure and upgrading zoning and building standards can guarantee the insurability of property risks" and concluded that, "[b]y working in partnership, insurers, governments and the private sector can address global challenges in a way that benefits everyone."[14]

In addition to transmitting information to insurers on relevant public works projects that reduce climate change risk, regulators can work with insurers to provide the public at large with information on how insurers value different mitigation strategies. This adaptation would increase awareness and transparency for resilience investments, facilitate competition on efficient underwriting for insurers, and create commercial opportunities.[15] The efforts of IBHS notwithstanding, at present, such information is lacking.[16] Regulators can also support the continuing development of public data to support better forecasts of climate change risk; this information is fundamental to actuarial modeling and pricing decisions for insurance, as well as for understanding the value of different mitigation strategies.

In areas in which insurance becomes burdensomely expensive for property owners due to risks driven by climate change, regulators can create or expand state-sponsored, high-risk insurance pools, such as FAIR plans, or beach and windstorm plans, such as those in Texas and Louisiana.[17] Referred to as *residual markets* in the insurance industry, such pools provide affordable insurance to property owners who otherwise cannot obtain insurance in the

---

[14] Swiss Re, "In a World of Growing Risk the Insurance Industry Has a Crucial Role to Play."

[15] Herweijer, Ranger, and Ward, "Adaptation to Climate Change."

[16] See, for example, Lachman et al., *Valuing Army Installation Resilience Investments for Natural Hazards.*

[17] According to the Insurance Information Institute, "Residual Markets,"

property insurance from the residual market is provided by Fair Access to Insurance Requirements (FAIR) Plans, Beach and Windstorm Plans, and two state-run insurance companies in Florida and Louisiana: Florida Citizens Property Insurance Corp. (CPIC) and Louisiana Citizens Property Insurance Corp. (Louisiana Citizens). Established in the late 1960s to ensure the continued provision of insurance in urban areas, FAIR Plans often provide property insurance in both urban and coastal areas, while Beach and Windstorm Plans cover predominantly wind-only risks in designated coastal areas. Hybrid plans, like Florida's and Louisiana's plans, provide property insurance throughout those states.

private market.[18] But, as risks increase, the policy goal of affordability conflicts with pricing policies such that they accurately reflect the likelihood of potential impacts for property owners. Consequently, state-sponsored high-risk pools often subsidize property owners for accepting risk, reducing their incentives to relocate or invest in resilience measures.[19]

To summarize, many strategies that mitigate climate change's consequences for property insurance markets require the insurer or reinsurer to respond to climate risk across all aspects of its business because insurance premiums and their responsiveness to resilience investments transmit information to policyholders. Regulators can work to support insurers in this arena by increasing the information available to both insurers and policyholders for decisionmaking. As climate change proceeds and property insurers exit high-risk areas, if markets incorporate mechanisms for accurate pricing and incentives to reduce risk, regulators can turn to the development or expansion of residual insurance markets to provide the needed coverage for property owners. The insurance adaptation strategy to value public and private infrastructure takes a long view: It can provide more social value if deployed before the frequency and severity of climate change hazards increase further. In contrast, state-sponsored high-risk insurance pools can be formed on a conditional, wait-and-see basis as a function of climate risk and market response.

Illustrative Examples of Risk Mitigation Practices

Although academics and industry experts urge action on climate change risk, illustrative examples and best practices for many of the mitigation strategies are still under development. Perhaps the easiest strategy for insurers and reinsurers is to manage their capital and underwriting with awareness of climate change risk. For example, McKinsey analysts advised that,

> Insurers should reevaluate their investment-allocation strategies as the economy transitions toward long-term decarbonization . . . [and] should also systematically evaluate the combined exposure of their investment and underwriting portfolios to physical climate risk, especially where both assets and liabilities could be affected.[20]

Informed by a survey of state regulators and interviews with personnel from rating agencies, environmental experts, and risk management experts, Deloitte Center for Financial Services offered these recommendations along these lines:

1. Raise the profile of climate risk in the organization.
2. Improve assessment of climate risk using advanced analytics.

---

[18] Center for Insurance Policy and Research, "Fair Access to Insurance Requirements (FAIR) Plans."

[19] See, for example, Craig, "Coastal Adaptation, Government-Subsidized Insurance, and Perverse Incentives to Stay"; and Hartwig and Wilkinson, *Residual Market Property Plans*.

[20] Grimaldi et al., "Climate Change and P&C Insurance."

3. Take an enterprise-wide view while managing climate risks.
4. Work with policyholders and policymakers to alleviate climate risk exposure.
5. Work with administrative agencies to develop climate-resilient public policies.[21]

Although the industry arguably has clear incentives to follow these practices over time, short-term profitability considerations could prevail and slow their implementation. A survey by the National Association of Insurance Commissioners (NAIC) indicated that less than 40 percent of property and casualty carriers altered their investment strategies in response to assessments of climate risk.[22]

To overcome this barrier, regulators could consider enacting environmental, social, and governance (ESG) policies that require reporting on the carbon impacts of underwriting and incentivize sustainable investment strategies.[23] Both the International Association of Insurance Supervisors (IAIS) and the Group of 20's Task Force on Climate-Related Financial Disclosures (TCFD) provide detailed guidance on how insurers should manage climate risk and make climate-related disclosures.[24] At their core, both the IAIS and the TCFD have called for a broad view of climate change risk assessed throughout the corporate structures of insurance and financial organizations, with disclosures reported in mainstream financial documents. Specifically, IAIS analysts made the following recommendations:

- Supervisors should assess the relevance of climate-related risks to their supervisory objectives. They should collect quantitative and qualitative information on the insurance sector's exposure to and management of physical, transition, and liability risks of climate change.
- Climate-related risks should be considered for inclusion in insurers' own risk and solvency assessments. It is expected that insurers will adopt appropriate risk management actions to mitigate any identified risks.
- Insurers should assess the impact that physical and transition risks could have on their investment portfolios, as well as on their asset–liability management. A forward-looking view, including the use of scenarios, could help insurers gain a better understanding of the risks.
- Material risks associated with climate change should be disclosed by insurers, in line with Insurance Core Principle 20 (Public Disclosure). Supervisors could use the TCFD's

---

[21] Deloitte Center for Financial Services, "Climate Risk."

[22] Groshong et al., *Assessment of and Insights from NAIC Climate Risk Disclosure Data.*

[23] For more information on ESG policies generally, see Gnanarajah and Shorter, "Introduction to Financial Services." ESG policies are a matter of political debate; see, e.g., Winston, "Why Business Leaders Must Resist the Anti-ESG Movement."

[24] IAIS, *Application Paper on the Supervision of Climate-Related Risks in the Insurance Sector*; TCFD, *Recommendations of the Task Force on Climate-Related Financial Disclosures.* In IAIS usage, *supervisor* refers to a market regulator akin to an insurance commissioner in the United States.

recommended framework when designing best practices or as input for setting their own supervisory objectives.[25]

Although the NAIC has endorsed the adoption of TCFD guidelines,[26] only the state of New York's Department of Financial Services has issued climate risk mitigation guidance for insurers, and no state requires insurance companies to report the carbon emissions of the companies they underwrite.[27]

Nonetheless, some illustrative models of how insurance companies might adapt to climate change risk do exist. The recent update to the National Flood Insurance Program's methodology for calculating premiums, referred to as *Risk Rating 2.0*, provides a case study in using detailed information to underwrite a climate change–related risk more accurately.[28] Although the adjustment of premiums arguably provides a better reflection of flood risk and, therefore, better incentives, policyholders have reacted to higher premiums with litigation: Ten states and several local governments have together filed a federal lawsuit to declare the Risk Rating 2.0 methodology unlawful.[29]

Elsewhere, Kahn, Casey, and Jones have pointed to Aviva and the United Services Automobile Association as examples of insurers that are using data on climate change–driven risks to inform premium calculations and discounts for at-risk homeowners.[30] Kahn, Casey, and Jones have also pointed to the evolution of the insurance-linked securities market and catastrophe (cat) bonds in particular. In brief, these financial instruments allow an alternative method to raise capital to pay claims should some well-specified extreme event occur within a defined time. Much like they are with an ordinary bond, investors are paid a risk-based rate of return over time and are repaid their principal when the bond comes to term if the extreme event does not occur. Although such bonds provide an attractive method for municipalities to hedge against climate change risk, they raise a moral-hazard concern: A municipality might choose to purchase a cat bond for insurance and then underinvest in resilient infrastructure. A recent partnership between re:focus and Swiss Re provides an illustrative example of how insurers can mitigate this issue: Drawing on modeling information from Risk Management Solutions, re:focus offers municipalities rebates on their cat bond costs for making resilience investments.[31]

---

[25] Bourtembourg et al., *The Impact of Climate Change on the Financial Stability of the Insurance Sector.*

[26] NAIC, "U.S. Insurance Commissioners Endorse Internationally Recognized Climate Risk Disclosure Standard for Insurance Companies."

[27] Fredman, "Regulators Should Identify and Mitigate Climate Risks in the Insurance Industry."

[28] National Flood Insurance Program, *Risk Rating 2.0 Methodology and Data Sources.*

[29] Amacher, "FEMA Hit by Multi-State Lawsuit over Flood Insurance Rating Formula."

[30] Kahn, Casey, and Jones, "How the Insurance Industry Can Push Us to Prepare for Climate Change."

[31] Vaijhala and Rhodes, "Resilience Bonds."

If private insurance becomes unavailable in some areas, states have many illustrative examples on which to draw to create high-risk insurance pools; indeed, many already are. Some form of FAIR plan exists in every state,[32] with total premiums written exceeding $3.8 billion for 2.2 million policies in 2021. Hartwig and Wilkinson provided details on the structures of eight of the largest residual programs and showed that they had grown rapidly over time: They cautioned that, absent land-use policies and incentives or regulations on building resilience investment, the subsidized premiums of these programs lead to increased risk for the pool.[33] Similarly, Born and Klein discussed best practices for setting property insurance premiums, with specific attention to residual markets. They emphasized that residual insurance markets can effectively manage risks but warned against overloading them with public policy goals—specifically, the affordability of coverage.[34] Finally, Molk pointed out that a hybrid public–private insurance market could offer some improvement, with public insurance playing the role of covering only the catastrophic portion of risk and leaving the remaining, more-typical losses to the private market.[35]

In summary, stakeholders can use either of two categories of strategies—those that reduce property's vulnerability to and effects from climate change and those that bolster or strengthen the insurance market's ability to accept these risks—to mitigate the risk of climate change to insurance markets (see Table 3.2). Strategies that reduce vulnerability can be implemented directly by property owners and their communities. Both insurers and state and local governments can deploy strategies that support the actions of property owners and their communities and, overall, mitigate climate change's consequences for the insurance market. For example, insurers can transmit the value of resilience investments by incorporating their impact on risk in premiums for property owners and then work to ensure that property owners have this information available. Similarly, insurers can work more closely with state and local governments to provide information on the value of resilient infrastructure for communities. In turn, federal, state, and local governments can ensure that insurance markets have the best information available for underwriting property risks. At the same time, insurers can provide additional capital for property insurance by expanding reinsurance or expanding the use of alternative capital, such as through the insurance-linked securities market. Regulators can encourage insurers to take these steps by increasing reporting requirements for climate change risks for insurers and reinsurers. Finally, state governments could consider developing new or expanding existing high-risk insurance pools to act as the property insurer of last resort, although this strategy has its own trade-offs.

---

[32] Center for Insurance Policy and Research, "Fair Access to Insurance Requirements (FAIR) Plans."

[33] Hartwig and Wilkinson, *Residual Market Property Plans.*

[34] Born and Klein, *Best Practices for Regulating Property Insurance Premiums and Managing Natural Catastrophe Risk in the United States.* Arguably, the adjustments made to the National Flood Insurance Program under Risk Rating 2.0 provide a case study of the realignment of a public insurance policy toward a truer reflection of the underlying risk (see, e.g., Horn, "National Flood Insurance Program Risk Rating 2.0").

[35] Molk, "The Government's Role in Climate Change Insurance."

TABLE 3.2

Summary of Climate Risk Mitigation Strategies for *Provide Insurance Services*

Risk Mitigation Strategy	Enabler	Barrier
Individual property owners or communities undertake adaptations to reduce the impacts of specific natural hazards (see Table 3.1).	Information and incentives that reflect the value of resilience investments	Lack of incentives for resilience investments, particularly in the form of premium discounts
Insurers provide information on the value of resilience investments to property owners or communities.	Best available data and models on natural hazards driven by climate change; reporting requirements for climate change risks	Institutional inertia, weak short-run economic incentives for insurers to respond to climate change
Federal, state, and local governments work with insurers to provide necessary data on existing and planned infrastructure to understand its impact on premiums and support insurance risk modeling.	Clear short-run incentives for insurers to incorporate climate change risks into decisionmaking	
Insurers provide additional capital for property insurance markets.		Competing demands for capital
State-level regulators mandate reporting on climate change risks for insurers and reinsurers (e.g., TCFD guidelines).	Development of appropriate guidelines, support for these guidelines at the national (e.g., the NAIC) and federal (e.g., the Federal Insurance Office) levels	Social and political resistance to ESG measures
State governments develop or expand high-risk property insurance pools.	Publicly developed and available models of underlying natural hazards that generate premiums accurately reflecting risks to property owners	Social concerns about the implicit subsidy to property owners in high-risk areas; moral hazard to live in high-risk areas; dampened price signal for resilience investments

CHAPTER 4

Prepare for and Manage Emergencies

National Critical Function Overview and Risk Due to Climate Change

Description of the National Critical Function

Prepare for and Manage Emergencies involves the ability to "organize and manage resources and responsibilities for dealing with all aspects of emergencies (prevent, protect, mitigate, respond, and recover), to be resilient to and reduce the harmful effects of all hazards."[1]

There are seven subfunctions associated with this NCF:[2]

- *Prepare for Emergencies*
- *Manage Emergencies*
- *Protect Against Threats and Hazards*
- *Prevent Attacks*
- *Mitigate Impacts of Threats and Hazards*
- *Respond to Incidents*
- *Recover from Incidents.*

Responsibility for this NCF exists at every level of government across diverse entities. Emergency management offices and associated staff facilitate work across subfunctions.[3] FEMA holds responsibility at the federal level, with a similar entity holding responsibility in each state, although the names of those entities vary (e.g., Montana Disaster and Emergency Services, Nevada Division of Emergency Management, New Mexico Department of Homeland Security and Emergency Management).

As important as efforts at the federal and state levels are for this NCF, the local level is where the primary responsibility and authority for this NCF lie. Every county in the United States must have a designated emergency manager, although that position is often not dedi-

---

[1] CISA, "National Critical Functions," 2020, p. 6.

[2] FEMA, "Mission Areas and Core Capabilities"; Silverman et al., *Why the Emergency Management Community Should Be Concerned About Climate Change.*

[3] Emergency Management Higher Education Project, "Principles of Emergency Management Supplement."

cated to emergency management on a full-time basis and might not be affiliated with a stand-alone office.[4] The number of emergency management staff at the county level varies significantly, with the majority of U.S. counties having two or fewer staff members.[5] In a local government of another kind (e.g., municipality, township, village), there might not be a designated emergency management office or emergency manager.

Where emergency management entities exist, the role of emergency management staff is not necessarily to directly carry out the work laid out in this NCF but instead, in many cases, to support the diverse entities across their jurisdictions in carrying out activities, such as hazard, vulnerability, and risk assessment; planning; training; exercises; or resource management.[6] Addressing the subfunctions of this NCF also requires the engagement of a variety of actors, including elected officials and representatives from first-response, public works and transportation, engineering, planning, finance, assessment, public health, education, and health care organizations.[7] These entities have the expertise, resources, and authority to do the work of preparedness, mitigation, response, recovery, prevention, and protection, although it takes the facilitation of emergency management staff to bring these entities together to think through and carry out these subfunctions effectively.[8]

Risk of Disruption Due to Climate Change

The effects of climate change are expected to lead to an increase in demand for emergency management support for extended periods because some seasonal natural hazards—such as wildfires—will likely occur outside their traditional seasons and multiple hazards will likely occur concurrently. Severe storm systems and flooding have the potential to cause widespread damage and destruction to homes, businesses, and other facilities, which, during acute events, can tax the emergency response and management systems with emergent fire, search-and-rescue, and medical responses. Extreme cold can lead to blizzards and ice storms, creating a need for snow clearance and assistance for vulnerable community members because of disrupted utilities and travel.[9] Extreme heat can lead to an increase in heat-related illnesses, including heart, lung, and kidney problems, increasing the need for acute emergency medical response and for emergency management support, such as planning and coordination

---

[4] McEntire, "Local Emergency Management Organizations"; Waugh and Tierney, *Emergency Management*; Weaver et al., "An Overview of a Demographic Study of United States Emergency Managers."

[5] National Association of Counties (NACo), "Managing Disasters at the County Level."

[6] Stanley and Waugh, "Emergency Managers for the New Millennium."

[7] Madrigano et al., "Beyond Disaster Preparedness."

[8] Jensen et al., "The County Emergency Manager's Role in Disaster Recovery"; Stanley and Waugh, "Emergency Managers for the New Millennium."

[9] Bolinger et al., "An Assessment of the Extremes and Impacts of the February 2021 South-Central U.S. Arctic Outbreak, and How Climate Services Can Help."

with public health agencies.[10] Wildfire can threaten homes, businesses, and other facilities, necessitating fire suppression, evacuation, and rescue. Drought can lead to an increase in the number and severity of dust storms.

Emergency management staff and their many partner organizations will have to collaborate in innovative ways to address these demands.[11] Although the COVID-19 pandemic was not climate-driven, the response led to a host of negative impacts related to the broader disaster management workforce (e.g., burnout, turnover, and retention difficulties) that might also result from the increased frequency and severity of climate-driven events.[12] Furthermore, general workforce shortages could also contribute to the risk of disruption. For example, wildland firefighting, fire services in rural areas, and emergency medical services (EMS) already face personnel shortages. The emergency management field more generally has faced these same staffing issues, and these challenges will likely grow with the increased risk of climate change.[13]

Subfunction Effects

Climate change will continue to drive an increase in the frequency and severity of climate drivers, which, in turn, will drive an increase in demand for action in the subfunctions *Prepare for Emergencies*, *Manage Emergencies*, *Protect Against Threats and Hazards*, *Mitigate Impacts of Threats and Hazards*, *Respond to Incidents*, and *Recover from Incidents*.[14] These increases will likely result in significant demand increases for this NCF and contribute to the inability to carry out all subfunctions effectively in some parts of the country. Fortunately, disruptions in these subfunctions will probably not occur simultaneously across most of the country. For these reasons, this NCF was assessed as being at risk of moderate disruption in coming decades.

Status of Risk Mitigation

Implementation of mitigation strategies to reduce climate-driven risk to this NCF is crucial at the local level because meeting the increased demand for the subfunctions is primarily a local responsibility. A small number of strategies that directly address climate risk by reduc-

---

[10] Seltenrich, "Between Extremes."

[11] Madrigano et al., "Beyond Disaster Preparedness."

[12] Marshall et al., "Natural and Manmade Disasters."

[13] Currie, *FEMA Workforce*; Gazzale, "Motivational Implications Leading to the Continued Commitment of Volunteer Firefighters"; Lantz and Runefors, "Recruitment, Retention and Resignation Among Non-Career Firefighters"; Sporer, "Burnout in Emergency Medical Technicians and Paramedics in the USA"; Wigglesworth, "Hellish Fires, Low Pay, Trauma."

[14] Reidmiller et al., *Impacts, Risks, and Adaptation in the United States.*

ing demand are widely in use (e.g., increase workforce, develop mutual-aid agreements).[15] For example, local staff establish mutual-aid agreements to establish the terms by which varying forms of assistance will be shared between local jurisdictions, and they devise preevent contracts to facilitate procurement of resources from the private sector.

Despite these efforts, the reality is that there is very little additional capacity to address climate risk mitigation specifically for this NCF at the local level, and there are several reasons for this, as we explain in the next section. This shortage of capacity does not mean that meaningful work related to this NCF is not occurring at the local level or that innovations involving this NCF cannot be found in some localities. However, local-level emergency management is not well positioned to engage in meaningful climate risk mitigation, and local-level governments need assistance to increase support for this NCF across the country in any significant or standardized way.

Barriers and Enablers of Risk Mitigation

There are several barriers to risk mitigation at the local level. First, the NCF is defined as being to "organize and manage resources and responsibilities for dealing with all aspects of emergencies" effectively.[16] However, local governments are often unprepared or unable to do so. Scholars have noted that emergency management staff facilitate less activity related to mitigation and recovery than to activity related to preparedness and response.[17] Scholars have also been critical of the emergency management field's performance on equity issues, access and functional needs, public participation, planning, use of information to aid in decisionmaking, and other areas.[18] As Stanley and Waugh noted, there is an "unevenness of capa-

---

[15] Lauland et al., *Strategies to Mitigate the Risk to the National Critical Functions Generated by Climate Change.*

[16] CISA, "National Critical Functions," 2020, p. 6.

[17] See, for example, Committee on Science, Engineering, and Public Policy and Committee on Increasing National Resilience to Hazards and Disasters, *Disaster Resilience*; Jensen and Kirkpatrick, "Local Emergency Management and Comprehensive Emergency Management (CEM)"; and Jensen and Kirkpatrick, "Local Recovery Coordinators and the National Disaster Recovery Framework."

[18] See, for example, Buchanan and Sparagowski, "The Role of Emerging Technologies and Social Justice in Emergency Management Practice"; Cooper, "Reflections on Engaging Socially Vulnerable Populations in Disaster Planning"; Ernst, LaDue, and Gerard, "Understanding Emergency Manager Forecast Use in Severe Weather Events"; Gershon et al., "Are Local Offices of Emergency Management Prepared for People with Disabilities?"; Horney, Naimi, et al., "Assessing the Relationship Between Hazard Mitigation Plan Quality and Rural Status in a Cohort of 57 Counties from 3 States in the Southeastern U.S."; Horney, Nguyen, et al., "Assessing the Quality of Rural Hazard Mitigation Plans in the Southeastern United States"; Olonilua, "Equity and Justice in Hazard Mitigation"; Roberts and Wernstedt, "Decision Biases and Heuristics Among Emergency Management Personnel"; Sullivan et al., "Do Hazard Mitigation Plans Represent the Resilience Priorities of Residents in Vulnerable Texas Coastal Counties?"; Wernstedt et al., "How Emergency Management Personnel (Mis?)Interpret Forecasts"; and Xiang, Gerber, and Zhang, "Language Access in Emergency and Disaster Preparedness."

bilities" at the local level in which "some [emergency management] agencies are well organized and capable, and others are not."[19]

Varying human capacity is a second reason for the dearth of mitigation efforts at the local level. Staffing in many local emergency management offices is inadequate to meet current demands. For example, in a recent study, NACo researchers found that small counties employ, on average, one full-time and one part-time employee with some responsibility for emergency management (i.e., they are often not dedicated solely to emergency management).[20] The same study showed that midsize counties employed three full-time staff and two part-time staff, on average, while large counties employed an average of nine full-time and one part-time staff.[21] The number of emergency management staff working at the local level in other types of jurisdictions (e.g., cities, villages, townships) is unknown. Before the pandemic, the emergency management field already faced the problem of an aging workforce.[22] Since the pandemic began, the field has faced additional morale, burnout, and turnover issues.[23] Without adequate numbers of staff, it is challenging for emergency management staff to fully address the needs of communities following a disaster.[24]

Capacity issues related to a variety of organizations in local government are well documented, particularly with respect to first-response organizations (see Chapter 5 for more detail).[25] Furthermore, as Stanley and Waugh pointed out,

> Local government has become more complex and fragmented. At best, departments do not work in concert; at worst, their objectives are at complete odds with one another. The emergency manager of tomorrow will be the catalyst to eliminate the incongruities between government agencies, operating not in isolation but in relation to all other departments and agencies within government.[26]

Acting as a catalyst is difficult if local emergency management is weak, either in the sense of the emergency management staff or in terms of those whose efforts they facilitate.[27]

---

[19] Stanley and Waugh, "Emergency Managers for the New Millennium," p. 766.

[20] NACo, "Managing Disasters at the County Level." This study defined *small county* as a county with a population of 50,000 or fewer, *medium county* as one with 50,000 to 500,000 people, and *large county* as one with 500,000 or more people (NACo, "Managing Disasters at the County Level").

[21] NACo, "Managing Disasters at the County Level."

[22] Eichorn, *Qualitative Exploratory Case Study.*

[23] See, for example, Merlo et al., "Engaged, Overextended, or Burned Out."

[24] McEntire, "Local Emergency Management Organizations."

[25] da Cruz, Rode, and McQuarrie, "New Urban Governance."

[26] Stanley and Waugh, "Emergency Managers for the New Millennium," p. 769.

[27] Madrigano et al., "Beyond Disaster Preparedness."

A third barrier to risk mitigation at the local level is that emergency management offices are faced with a variety of climate drivers that differ by location.[28] Offices must comply with varying requirements stemming from state law, local ordinances, and grants.[29] Fulfillment of these requirements does not ensure that activity in all subfunctions is supported; instead, the requirements can put staff in a reactive stance and require time and effort to be met.[30] Funding for emergency management is not standardized across localities, and local emergency management is generally described as underresourced.[31] The level of the public's and elected officials' commitment to emergency management varies so much that Sylves labeled it a "perennial problem."[32] The fact that emergency management staff across the country have unequal knowledge across functional areas and lack familiarity with empirically based approaches to practice across areas also has an impact on what work is undertaken with respect to each subfunction.[33]

Despite these barriers, some approaches are used to facilitate emergency management and create more consistency and collaboration across offices. All states and territories are members of the Emergency Management Assistance Compact, which provides a mechanism through which states can borrow human and materiel response and recovery resources from other states and territories and reimburse associated costs. Within states, incident management teams are trained, mobilized, and deployed to augment the staff of local emergency management offices during severe or long-duration events. Community emergency response teams, made up of denizens who are trained in basic first response and emergency management, are leveraged by local emergency management staff to supplement local needs during hazard events. In many localities, volunteer first responders are counted on to provide basic emergency services.

An entity at the federal, state, or territorial level can provide funding, information, technical support, and other resources to support local entities as they try to address the subfunctions for this NCF. Yet entities at these levels cannot carry out activities across subfunctions at the local level. They lack the responsibility, authority, and local knowledge to do so effectively, and they do not own local resources.[34] Should an entity at the federal, state, or territorial level

---

[28] Jensen and Ferreira, "An Exploration of Local Emergency Management Program Accreditation Pursuit."

[29] Jensen and Ferreira, "An Exploration of Local Emergency Management Program Accreditation Pursuit."

[30] Jensen and Ferreira, "An Exploration of Local Emergency Management Program Accreditation Pursuit."

[31] Dzigbede, Gehl, and Willoughby, "Disaster Resiliency of U.S. Local Governments"; McEntire, "Local Emergency Management Organizations"; NACo, "Managing Disasters at the County Level"; Sylves, *Disaster Policy and Politics*, p. 26.

[32] Sylves, *Disaster Policy and Politics*, p. 18.

[33] See, for example, Jensen et al., "The County Emergency Manager's Role in Disaster Recovery"; Jensen and Kirkpatrick, "Local Emergency Management and Comprehensive Emergency Management (CEM)"; McCreight and Harrop, "Uncovering the Real Recovery Challenge"; Williams, "Understanding Where Emergency Management Gets the Knowledge to Solve the Problems They Face."

[34] Sylves, *Disaster Policy and Politics*.

pursue purposeful implementation of climate risk mitigation strategies for this NCF and its subfunctions, its actions cannot substitute for the lack of the same at the local level.

Illustrative Examples of Risk Mitigation Practices

Although we identified only a few existing risk mitigation practices beyond the limited strategies discussed in the research team's other report,[35] we did identify additional evidence-based approaches that might reduce the impact that climate-driven risk could have for this NCF in both direct and indirect ways. We discuss these in this section, focusing first on strategies that apply to federal, state, and territorial actors and then on strategies for local actors.

Direct Mitigation Strategies: Federal, State, and Territorial Actors

It is worth considering what types of direct mitigation strategies might make meaningful change for the barriers discussed earlier in this chapter. A host of strategies that focus on either (1) supporting some increase in the size and capacity of the emergency management workforce or (2) making the emergency management system more efficient would generate reductions in risk, if implemented. Yet, because control over implementation of those strategies lies with legislators and agencies at the federal, state, and territorial levels, such strategies rely on political cooperation that might be difficult to harness.

For example, one strategy is to **significantly increase the amount of funding available to support entities at the local level in carrying out the subfunctions associated with this NCF day to day**. The federal government routinely provides various sources of funding to state and local governments to support reducing or eliminating the impacts from natural hazards (e.g., the Building Resilient Communities and Infrastructure grant program; flood mitigation assistance); opportunities to increase funding at that level should continue to be pursued in conjunction with ways to reduce the burden on locals in accessing those funds. Funding streams specific to reducing or eliminating the impact of natural hazards could also be developed at the state level; an example is Arkansas's Hazard Mitigation Grant Program. Another transformational strategy would be to significantly increase funding appropriated to preparedness grants to support hiring more emergency management staff at the local level. Such a strategy could indicate the minimum number of full-time dedicated emergency management staff needed according to jurisdictional population size, vulnerability indicators, or other criteria, which might be considered in exchange for access to funding and could also include baseline emergency management–specific education and training requirements of any emergency management staff. These actions would mitigate risk to the NCF by increasing capacity to address all subfunctions in an evidence-based manner at a minimum level

---

[35] Lauland et al., *Strategies to Mitigate the Risk to the National Critical Functions Generated by Climate Change.*

across the country. Requiring preevent recovery planning or the development of memorandums of understanding (MOUs), memorandums of agreement (MOAs), or contracts to secure needed support and resources over the course of recovery would support enhanced readiness to address this subfunction in the future. There is currently no federal requirement to engage in preevent recovery planning, and research has revealed that agreements and contracts to support recovery are lacking.[36] Mandating these activities, perhaps as an attachment to grant funding, does not eliminate the sources of climate-driven risk, but it does help local jurisdictions become more efficient in dealing with recovery from the events they will experience.

As another example, **the federal government could articulate what an emergency management program that addresses all subfunctions effectively would entail to facilitate consistency state to state and across the country.** The emergency management field at SLTT levels currently lacks consensus on this topic, and, in the absence of consensus, emergency management personnel continue to take a reactive stance, addressing what is required or due next, regardless of whether that task is most important or valuable. With a clear articulation of the requirements of a holistic emergency management program, the federal government could assess current regulations and grant requirements in light of that picture and could eliminate or simplify anything that does not contribute significantly to the most-crucial aspects of a holistic emergency management program. Barnosky and his colleagues provided recommendations on what might be eliminated or simplified, even in the absence of articulation of a holistic emergency management program.[37]

New education and training requirements, such as those previously mentioned, might also be developed to support emergency management staff in delivering such a program. Additionally, a clear articulation of program requirements could be leveraged to focus and streamline emergency management education and training.[38] These changes would not reduce climate-driven risk to this NCF but would help local jurisdictions become more efficient in dealing with related increased demands.

Pursuit of these ideas would be costly. Bringing these ideas to fruition would require a level of consensus and willingness to invest in emergency management at the federal level, and potentially also at the state and territorial levels, that has not previously existed. Changes in law, appropriations, regulation, and policy would be required. Bringing about these changes might not be possible. The reality is that reducing climate-driven risk to this NCF defies easy solution.

---

[36] International City/County Management Association, "Disaster Resilience and Recovery Survey."

[37] Barnosky et al., *Streamlining Emergency Management.*

[38] Jensen and Kirkpatrick, "Local Emergency Management and Comprehensive Emergency Management (CEM)."

Direct Mitigation Strategies: Local Actors

It might well be that the mitigation options that the emergency management community can feasibly implement are those that can be initiated in the short term and require only local implementation. Strategies that fall into this category are primarily those that involve **doing current work more efficiently or effectively** to reduce future demand for one or more subfunctions. There is no shortage of mitigation strategies along these lines, and they are most feasible in the short term because each could conceivably be implemented at the local level without federal, state, or territorial action.

It is likely that such strategies will be implemented inconsistently, at best, and would therefore lead to only partial, nontransformational change. As discussed previously, local jurisdictions vary widely in the following ways, among others:

- funding to support subfunctions associated with this NCF
- the number of available emergency management staff, as well as their knowledge and skills
- legislated job duties for the local emergency management office
- buy-in from local elected officials and the public
- the capacity of local actors who are needed to support the work associated with this NCF
- the organizational placement of the emergency management function within the jurisdiction
- technology access.

These factors will all influence the feasibility of implementing these types of mitigation strategies in positive or negative ways.

Furthermore, federal, state, or territorial action would enable more-widespread implementation. Nevertheless, in the context of mounting climate-driven risk, it is important to implement as many mitigation strategies as possible. See Table 4.1 for examples of mitigation strategies that are implementable at the local level in the short term, along with discussion of what would enable implementation.

Indirect Strategies

Given the pathway or relationship of climate risk drivers to this NCF, the first, and by far the most impactful, strategy is to **alleviate future increases in demand for this NCF by reducing vulnerability to hazard events at the local level across the United States** (e.g., addressing root causes related to disasters [such as addressing social and environmental injustice], reducing the likelihood of flooding through mitigation measures [such as levees, changed building codes, or zoning], or reducing likelihood of wildfire by changing building codes or zoning). Another meaningful approach would be to increase support for this NCF by ensuring the implementation of mitigation strategies for the NCFs on which *Prepare for and Manage Emergencies* relies (e.g., *Provide Wireless Access Network Services, Provide Wireline Access Network Services, Provide Satellite Access Network Services, Distribute Elec-*

TABLE 4.1

Summary of Climate Risk Mitigation Strategies for *Prepare for and Manage Emergencies*

Risk Mitigation Strategy	Enabler	Barrier
Ensure that local governments regularly engage in scenario-based planning and develop exercises to test jurisdictional readiness.	Support from FEMA in the form of technical assistance, templates of scenarios, and other training, along with funding for time spent	Insufficient staff capacity and resources at the local level
Ensure the inclusion of underserved communities in planning efforts.	Robust, easily accessible training on effective participation techniques	Possible lack of prior relationships, buy-in, or support from underserved communities
Provide the public with access to emergency response plans.	Federal, state, or territorial laws, regulations, or policy being updated to recommend or require public posting of emergency response plans and dissemination to local actors	Reluctance by federal and SLTT actors to share information deemed sensitive or secure
Gather data and conduct analysis on underserved communities to inform grant programs.	Existing guidance for grant programs being expanded and clarified about the extent to which hazard identification and risk management should include underserved communities and how; federal, state, or territorial entities providing accessible training on how to conduct effective hazard identification and risk management processes and how to use the data from those processes to inform a variety of activities across the subfunctions associated with this NCF	Long timelines and need for buy-in from political leaders to engage in legislative changes or rulemaking
Give local jurisdictions free access to communication technologies and training on how to use them.	State and territorial entities providing local jurisdictions access to various technologies and allowing or encouraging additional local actors to be granted full or limited access at no cost	Funding challenges, as well as insufficient staff capacity, to adopt new technologies and undertake necessary training
Build relationships with nongovernmental organizations and involve them in planning activities.	Federal, state, or territorial entities making robust training on nongovernmental organizations easily accessible to local jurisdictions	Possible lack of prior relationships, buy-in, or support from these organizations
Facilitate the mitigation strategies outlined for the *Provide Public Safety* NCF.	(See Chapter 5.)	(See Chapter 5.)

Table 4.1—Continued

Risk Mitigation Strategy	Enabler	Barrier
Conduct predisaster planning at the local level.	Federal, state, or territorial entities supplementing existing guidance by making recovery planning training, templates, or example plans available and easily accessible	Insufficient staff capacity and resources at the local level
Develop MOAs, MOUs, and procurement contracts for recovery.	Federal, state, or territorial entities identifying and sharing potential contract needs for recovery and templates or example contracts to support local implementation	MOAs and MOUs not reflecting the diversity of incident types and local contexts throughout the country, thereby leading them to not be adopted or worsening problems they aim to solve

NOTE: This table includes only strategies that could be implemented locally in the short term.

tricity). For example, if climate-driven impact on water and energy sources can be mitigated, fewer people and community lifelines will require assistance, which will reduce demand for response and recovery efforts within emergency management. This approach would ensure that entities involved in *Prepare for and Manage Emergencies* have the resources and infrastructure required to address subfunctions efficiently and effectively. For this reason, focusing on mitigation strategies in other related NCFs is the most important mitigation strategy for *Prepare for and Manage Emergencies*.

CHAPTER 5

Provide Public Safety

National Critical Function Overview and Risk Due to Climate Change

Description of the National Critical Function

The *Provide Public Safety* NCF is made up of "public services—to include police, fire, and emergency medical services—to ensure the safety and security of communities, businesses, and populations."[1] It has six subfunctions:

- *Contribute to Law Enforcement*
- *Provide Fire and Rescue Services*
- *Provide EMS*
- *Provide Public Works Support*
- *Provide Emergency Management*
- *Support Public Health Services.*

Significant overlap exists between this NCF's mission and workforce and those of *Enforce Law* and *Prepare for and Manage Emergencies.*[2] Many of the risks and mitigation strategies discussed in Chapter 4 are therefore explained in that chapter.

Although this NCF includes actions and functions across all levels of government, most of the country's capacity for this NCF and its component subfunctions is situated at the local level. For example, the primary actors responsible for the *Provide Fire and Rescue Services* subfunction in the United States are registered fire and rescue departments, and 96 percent

---

[1] CISA, "National Critical Functions," 2020, p. 6.

[2] This overlap extends to the designation of certain NCFs as subfunctions of others, complicating the organization of this construct. This can be seen in the similarity in both name and definition of the *Provide Emergency Management* subfunction and the *Prepare for and Manage Emergencies* NCF or the *Provide Public Works Support* subfunction and the variety of public works–related NCFs. This overlap turns back on itself upon examination of these connected NCFs, creating a feedback loop that might undercut their use in organizing thought and decisionmaking on these topics. For instance, the *Prepare for and Manage Emergencies* NCF has subfunctions for *Respond to Incidents* and *Recover from Incidents*, both of which describe actors and activities matching the six subfunctions of *Provide Public Safety*. Similar overlap exists between the *Provide Public Safety* subfunction *Contribute to Law Enforcement* and the *Enforce Law* NCF.

of these are local departments.[3] Although most capacity for this NCF is based in local government, private components also exist, mostly in the *Provide EMS* subfunction, in which an estimated 22 percent of agencies are either for-profit or nonprofit entities, often contracted with local jurisdictions.[4] Local actors' work to manage the NCF actors is supplemented and augmented through additional regional, state, and federal departments, as well as neighboring localities, through automatic or mutual-aid agreements.

In addition to capacity, true control over the organization and fulfillment of this NCF and its subfunctions rests largely at the local level. In fact, many of the subfunctions of this NCF fall quite explicitly under the core examples of "police power" described in U.S. Supreme Court decisions, a power that legal scholars generally acknowledge as reserved for states per the Tenth Amendment.[5] Despite the fact that federalization has progressed at varying rates for all these police powers,[6] authority for providing them still rests largely with the states and, through delegation from them, localities. This point about authority and control is fundamental to assessing potential strategies for dealing with any risk to this NCF and its subfunctions. In many cases, federal efforts to address that risk will be made up largely of supporting and coordinating efforts—large federal presences through such responsibility and authority as federal wildland firefighting, law enforcement, or public health guidance notwithstanding.

The departments responsible for this NCF at all SLTT levels, across all subfunctions, face long-standing challenges in building and maintaining sufficient workforces to meet current demand.[7] As a result, the departments are left vulnerable to shocks and stresses from a variety of climate drivers. These climate drivers, many of which are anticipated to increase in frequency or severity, can be expected to exacerbate staffing issues by making the work of this NCF more dangerous and more difficult—increasingly frequent hot days carry with them uncomfortable conditions and deep health risks for firefighters, for example, raising worries about the danger of already-risky work[8]—while also placing the facilities and physical presence of the responsible agencies at direct risk. Additionally, a large amount of the country's emergency response capacity lies with such entities as the National Guard, which is often made up of the same emergency responders that National Guard activation is meant to support—up to one-third of National Guard members in one study worked in such roles

---

[3] U.S. Fire Administration, "National Fire Department Registry Quick Facts."

[4] MacKenzie and Carlini, *Characterizing Local EMS Systems.*

[5] *Berman v. Parker*, 1954; Congressional Research Service, "Amdt10.3.2 State Police Power and Tenth Amendment Jurisprudence."

[6] J. Baker, "State Police Powers and the Federalization of Local Crime."

[7] Currie, *FEMA Workforce*; Keenan, "The Shortfall of Qualified Applicants and the Generational Implications That Impact Law Enforcement"; Kintziger et al., "The Impact of the COVID-19 Response on the Provision of Other Public Health Services in the U.S."; Wigglesworth, "Hellish Fires, Low Pay, Trauma."

[8] H. Smith and Mejia, "Extreme Heat Waves Are Making L.A. Firefighters Sick, Adding New Dangers to Job."

as law enforcement or health care[9]—meaning that some amount of backup staffing is double counted.

Risk of Disruption Due to Climate Change

Provide Public Safety is vulnerable to climate change because of expected increases in the frequency, intensity, or duration of the climate drivers that will put increased pressure on the NCF. Tropical cyclones, severe storm systems, and floods, all exacerbated by sea-level rise, have the capacity to cause widespread damage or destruction to homes, businesses, and other facilities. Extreme cold, particularly when paired with winter storms, can cause injuries and deaths from traffic accidents, as well as from hypothermia, particularly among people who are older or experiencing poverty, who often have inadequate heat. Extreme heat can cause an increase in heat-related illnesses, including heart, lung, and kidney problems, as well as issues with fetal health. Some studies have also shown that hotter weather is correlated with an increase in crime and terrorist attacks; less clear is whether there is a causal relationship and, if so, what the magnitude of that effect is.[10] High energy usage associated with heat waves can cause blackouts and damage to power transmission facilities. Wildfires can threaten homes, businesses, and other facilities, necessitating fire suppression, evacuation, and rescue, while smoke from those fires causes additional harm, including potentially acting as an infectious-disease vector.[11] Drought can lead to an increase in the frequency of dust storms, which, in turn, can exacerbate respiratory diseases.

Together, the effects of climate change are expected to affect demand for this NCF and its workforce. Specifically, climate change will likely increase the need for law enforcement to maintain order, fire services to suppress fires and provide rescue, and EMS to provide prehospital care—service providers who will also need to help conduct evacuations and support displaced people. During large disasters, emergency management personnel will need to coordinate with public health personnel, while restoration of damaged utilities will require support from public works.[12] The effects of climate change could also contribute to workforce shortages. For example, the United States currently faces a shortage of wildland firefighters, and this shortage could grow as the threat of wildfires increases.[13]

---

[9] Allison-Aipa et al., "The Impact of National Guard Activation for Homeland Defense."

[10] Abbott, "An Uncertain Future"; Goin, Rudolph, and Ahern, "Impact of Drought on Crime in California."

[11] Kobziar and Thompson, "Wildfire Smoke, a Potential Infectious Agent."

[12] Calma, "Texas' Natural Gas Production Just Froze Under Pressure."

[13] A. Phillips, "It's California Wildfire Season"; Quinton, "Lack of Federal Firefighters Hurts California Wildfire Response"; Safo, "U.S. Fire Service Is Short Thousands of Firefighters amid Pay Raise Delay."

Subfunction Effects

This risk of increased demand is spread across subfunctions in uneven ways. For example, the pathway to increased probabilities of drought and heat causing longer and severer wildfire seasons is a clear one that shows a likely-direct increase in demand for *Provide Fire and Rescue Services*. Similarly clear pathways exist for other subfunctions, such as that same increase in heat pushing up demand for *Provide EMS* due to heat-related health emergencies or increasing strain on *Support Public Health Services* by necessitating cooling centers and heat-management activities.[14] However, the same climate driver can also create an increase in demand for other subfunctions through less obvious pathways, such as increases in crime rates during heat events building demand for *Contribute to Law Enforcement*.[15]

To a significant degree, climate's effects on this NCF are indirect and mitigated through cascading effects from other NCFs. For example, all subfunctions of *Provide Public Safety* rely on stable, functioning communication networks to operate at full force and efficiency. Therefore, any effect on *Provide Wireless Access Network Services*, *Provide Wireline Access Network Services*, or *Provide Satellite Access Network Services* would reduce actors' ability to fulfill their missions under *Provide Public Safety*. Additionally, failures in some NCFs can cause disruptions to public safety that necessitate response from the entities responsible for *Provide Public Safety*. For instance, even localized failures for *Distribute Electricity* or *Transmit Electricity*, which could result from damaging, severe weather or burden during a heat event, can create serious risk to health and safety for vulnerable populations, placing strain on the *Provide EMS* subfunction that exceeds a jurisdiction's capacity. Through such a hypothetical yet very plausible scenario, a pathway of dependence can be drawn from *Provide EMS* to the resilience of private utility enterprises that operate hundreds of miles away. A similar level of interconnectedness exists between this NCF and a wide variety of others, making *Provide Public Safety* particularly vulnerable to any disruptions in other critical functions at local, regional, and even national levels.

Status of Risk Mitigation

Mitigation activities for this NCF can be classified as those addressing the supply side of public safety provision rather than the demand for it caused by the cascading effects stemming from disruptions to other NCFs.

There are a variety of potential mitigation options to address supply-side issues related to the stable provision of this NCF. Yet, given the long-standing nature of staffing problems across all subfunctions related to this NCF, these options might appear deceptively simple. Strategies to augment staffing, such as building volunteer reserve corps, seem viable as a means of augmenting professional departments, but the subfunction *Provide Fire and Rescue*

---

[14] Seltenrich, "Between Extremes."

[15] Abbott, "An Uncertain Future"; Goin, Rudolph, and Ahern, "Impact of Drought on Crime in California."

Services is already heavily reliant on volunteers. Because more than 85 percent of the country's fire departments are mostly or entirely volunteer, there might not be significant numbers of volunteers available to serve in a reserve corps. Likewise, developing and exercising mutual-aid agreements is a best practice across the United States now. Although this is a tactic that should be preserved and expanded, it cannot be expected to provide more than a modicum of additional risk mitigation, given that its use is already widespread.

With these enduring challenges, transformational change might be needed to truly mitigate climate risk. Aside from traditional models to boost employee recruitment and retention, such transformational thinking might entail such models as compulsory service or medium-term employment modeled on military service. Some countries have implemented models in which denizens may serve in police, fire, EMS, and rescue roles to fulfill their required service. The United States might investigate these existing models and consider the extent to which a similar design might benefit it. Because recruitment and retention are already challenges in these occupational areas, we recommend that a term of service similar in length to the uniformed branches' enlistment periods, with comparable scholarship and postservice benefits, be considered as a component of any design pursued.

Such a national service model would be difficult to implement and, by its nature, would boost staffing levels in a way that increases already-high rates of turnover in the subfields responsible for this NCF. However, building it would provide a large and stable pipeline of guaranteed staff to these frontline agencies while allowing the local control inherent to the country's public safety systems. This idea might also be viable for individual states or regional consortia of states.

For the preservation and expansion of existing cooperative agreements across jurisdictions and levels of government, the same level of rethinking might be in order. Certain levels of efficiency can be gained in ensuring modularity and interchangeability between regions and entities. That modularity and interchangeability can facilitate the cooperation sought through these agreements. In some subfunctions—notably, *Provide Fire and Rescue Services*—this modularity already exists; standardized firefighting qualifications and widespread adoption of the National Incident Management System mean that a wildland firefighter might routinely flow between incidents managed at federal, state, and local levels regardless of their home agency or region. The same efficiencies of scale from modularity can be gained in other subfunctions through such policies as national EMS certifications with automatic state-level reciprocity or consistent and standardized organizational systems for public health and emergency management in each state.

Finally, because the outcomes and delivery of each subfunction in this NCF are so localized, those subfunctions' effects and stresses will also be local, or perhaps regional, in nature. Climate hazards do not respect geographic boundaries, and this fact can stand as a risk (large events might affect neighbors who would otherwise be willing to help) or a benefit (capacity can come from far-off, unaffected regions, as is the case with many Gulf Coast hurricanes or major wildfires). This reality means that mitigating activity in the form of increased cooperation and resource-sharing among the country's responsible public safety agencies and entities could be beneficial.

Many of the subfunctions that fall under *Provide Public Safety* are the subjects of social and political conversations much larger than climate change risk mitigation. Nationwide protests over the role and nature of law enforcement in life in the United States and postpandemic mistrust of public health policy and officials loom as two notable examples of those conversations that are already driving change in how these subfunctions are delivered around the country. Although such an atmosphere of tension and rapid change does not necessarily make any of the mitigation strategies discussed here less impactful or important, it might make some of them less viable. Massive increases in the budgets and manpower to support national service models aimed at increasing staff in the face of growing demand might not win the needed buy-in from political leaders or voters already questioning the sizes of police budgets or the levels of authority granted to public health actors during emergencies.

Illustrative Examples of Risk Mitigation Practices

As stated above, a variety of both supply- and demand-side pathways exist to reduce climate risk to this NCF. Although some are already utilized to varying extents across the United States, others stand as ambitious changes to the way the subfunctions of *Provide Public Safety* are delivered and might not be feasible or realistic in the current political climate. These mitigation strategies reiterate calls in the Lauland et al. report while offering potential pathways to achieving them. The strategies discussed in this section, therefore, share the same high levels of feasibility for addressing climate risks to the NCF and depend on funding, labor market conditions, and lengthy political processes to implement. All these strategies focus directly on *Provide Public Safety* and its component subfunctions, aiming to improve their capacities through expanded workforces and cooperation.

These illustrative examples of ways to address this NCF's supply-side concerns consist of developing national volunteer auxiliaries, increasing the modularity and cross-compatibility of subfunction staff, and developing a national service model that feeds temporary employees directly into locally managed agencies responsible for subfunctions.

Implementing National Volunteer Auxiliaries

National volunteer auxiliaries tap the long-standing and widespread use of volunteer labor in certain subfunctions—namely, *Provide Fire and Rescue Services* and *Provide EMS*—and uses it as a model for other subfunctions. Such attempts to augment professional public safety staff with volunteers have been implemented widely and shown to produce some favorable outcomes.[16] The idea, like others described here, is scalable and could be implemented at a

---

[16] Kang, "Volunteer Involvement and Organizational Performance."

national, state, or even local level. Examples of this model exist in many jurisdictions: Los Angeles County Public Works has a Public Works Volunteer Program, for instance.[17] Such an idea can be expanded to include roles filled on a more emergent basis, such as repairing infrastructure or clearing debris after a major climate event. A potential downside to this idea is that it relies on a spirit of volunteerism that might wane based on certain factors, such as household employment rates or shifting cultural priorities. Finally, to the extent that the work of national volunteer auxiliaries can be demonstrated to reduce the impacts of natural disasters, property insurers might take notice and offer rate reductions in areas where they are present. We do not observe this practice at present and therefore cannot estimate the magnitude of potential savings, but they might offer a benefit that could defray some of the costs of supporting these units.

Increasing the Modularity of Staff

An attempt to increase the modularity of staff and resources for these subfunctions across jurisdictional lines can build on existing efforts. For example, the national EMS Compact is an attempt to build such modularity into the *Provide EMS* subfunction by developing a standing reciprocity agreement to grant certified emergency medical providers the privilege to practice and has, to some level, been established in more than 20 states.[18] Similar efforts to expand reciprocity in peace officer standards and training can create modular systems for *Contribute to Law Enforcement*, licensure recognition for key roles in public works management, and certification transfer for public health officials. Although expanding reciprocity requires state-level legislative and regulatory efforts, there has been some level of progress toward national reciprocity for relevant certifications across all subfunctions of this NCF. Again, this type of idea could be implemented at any level, with increased cooperation among localities standing as a possibility alongside more–nationally coordinated efforts, such as an expansion of such efforts as the Emergency Management Assistance Compact. Additionally, advances in communication technology or even automation might allow a modular workforce to be managed remotely. Although such a remote workforce might be less viable for EMS or fire responses, certain law enforcement and public health operations, as well as the support activities behind all public safety responses, could be supported by workers far from the direct service area.

Creating a National Service Model

Perhaps most ambitiously, a national service model could expand the pool of workers for the subfunctions of *Provide Public Safety* from local labor markets and available volunteers to entire generations. Even if implemented as a voluntary model akin to modern military

---

[17] Los Angeles County Public Works, "Public Works Volunteer Program."

[18] Interstate Commission for EMS Personnel Practice, "What Is the EMS Compact?"

recruiting and service, this model could include thousands of rural law enforcement officers, wildland firefighters, urban ambulance staff, and public health professionals. Although international examples of such a system exist, national service models in the United States have largely been restricted to wartime military drafts and male registration for the Selective Service System, making this an option as unfamiliar to policymakers and the public as it is ambitious in scope. Although such a service model relies on the economies of scale brought at the national level, it can also be replicated in individual states and can be tied to tuition benefits for higher-education institutions as a hypothetical example of GI Bill–style incentives for participation.[19] Such an idea might help provide qualified staff in areas that have difficulty recruiting and retaining it—namely, remote, rural, or underresourced jurisdictions that, under current conditions, lose bidding wars for police officers, firefighters, emergency medical technicians, emergency managers, and public health professionals to larger and wealthier locales.

Demand-side pathways to reducing climate risk are less clear and largely controlled by other NCFs. For instance, disaster preparedness and mitigation activities serving the *Provide Emergency Management* subfunction are addressed in, and organized under, the discussion of *Prepare for and Manage Emergencies* in Chapter 4. To a similar extent, this pattern exists for mitigating activities under the *Enforce Law* NCF as risk reduction for the *Contribute to Law Enforcement* subfunction and under *Develop and Maintain Public Works and Services* or similar NCFs and the *Provide Public Works Support* subfunction.

In summation, the strategies offered here rank highly in terms of technological, environmental, and geophysical feasibility and, if implemented, would help to address the supply-side concerns faced for all subfunctions of *Provide Public Safety* as the NCF experiences increasing demand brought on by climate drivers. However, each strategy is less feasible in economic, institutional, and social terms, requiring substantial funding investments and buy-in from key political and social actors. Table 5.1 summarizes the risk mitigation strategies for the *Provide Public Safety* NCF.

---

[19] *GI Bill* is shorthand for Public Law 78-346, Servicemen's Readjustment Act of 1944.

TABLE 5.1

Summary of Climate Risk Mitigation Strategies for *Provide Public Safety*

Risk Mitigation Strategy	Enabler	Barrier
National volunteer auxiliaries can expand the long-standing use of volunteers in this NCF's subfunctions to a more organized system that taps a larger pool of potential volunteers.	Favorable labor market conditions; licensing reciprocity across jurisdictions; acceptance of volunteers in roles typically reserved for full staff	Tight labor markets; a general unwillingness to volunteer in these roles
Increasing the modularity of staff and resources across the subfunctions of this NCF and boosting mutual-aid agreements can even out capacity differences across jurisdictions and help lessen the effects of large incidents that might overwhelm local resources.	Political efforts across all levels of SLTT partner governments to implement the licensure-reciprocity agreements and of mutual-aid agreements	Unwillingness of state and local governments to cooperate on reciprocity and mutual-aid agreements
The development of a national service model, or smaller state-level versions of one, focused on this NCF's subfunctions can create a consistent and stable workforce pipeline to meet increasing demand.	Political effort; substantial funding; efforts to build public support	Public aversion to a mandatory service model; insufficient political will to implement one; inadequate funding

CHAPTER 6

Conclusion

Climate change poses a variety of risks to the NCFs and associated critical infrastructure across the United States, including, in the most-extreme cases, the risk of disruption. In previous research, we assessed this risk to the 55 NCFs using a present-day baseline and two future periods: 2050 and 2100. This assessment has provided an understanding of which NCFs are at greatest risk due to climate change and included details about the climate drivers (e.g., drought, extreme heat) of that risk for each NCF. In addition to conducting the risk assessment, we examined how NCFs have mitigated and could mitigate the risk of disruption posed by climate change.

This report has detailed our complementary analysis of risk mitigation for four NCFs— *Maintain Supply Chains, Provide Insurance Services, Prepare for and Manage Emergencies,* and *Provide Public Safety*—that span a broad set of infrastructure assets and services and are of high interest to CISA. For each NCF, we provided an overview of the risks posed by climate change, described the status of climate risk mitigation, and presented a set of example strategies that have been or could be implemented to further reduce risks.

As a group, these four NCFs offer insights into how to think about the challenges of risk mitigation:

- *Maintain Supply Chains* is a complex and widespread NCF with no singular actor or geographic concentration but with many potential choke points for disruption. This reality makes risk mitigation a diffuse activity that is difficult to centralize or assess for efficacy.
- *Prepare for and Manage Emergencies* and *Provide Public Safety* are two NCFs with high degrees of activity at local levels: Local emergency responders and public safety officials are on the front lines of dealing with the effects of climate change. This fact means that risk mitigation must address the diverse needs of localities to meet the challenges resulting from more-frequent or severer climate drivers in the future.
- Mitigating risk for *Provide Insurance Services* depends both on direct activities to shore up vulnerabilities in the insurance market and on indirect activities that mitigate insurance-covered risks, such as flooding and hurricanes.
- Notably, these NCFs are affected by community preparedness and hazard mitigation investments that might be implemented by other NCFs' stakeholders, a fact that exem-

plifies how risk mitigation investments in upstream NCFs could generate dividends for other NCFs.

- In addition, the latter three NCFs— *Provide Insurance Services, Prepare for and Manage Emergencies,* and *Provide Public Safety*—are not as widely covered in the climate adaptation literature and do not have significant asset footprints, and this fact suggests the need for a better understanding of these sectors' climate risk mitigation requirements.

Key Takeaways

Given these complexities, some key takeaways can be derived from our examination of risk mitigation among this group of NCFs.

The NCF framework can be a useful lens through which to consider climate adaptation. Governments, communities, and critical infrastructure owners and operators find themselves under increasing risk as a result of climate change. Given the broad scope of risk from climate change, any opportunity to identify additional viable means of mitigating this risk is likely to be valuable. Traditional approaches to critical infrastructure are focused on physical assets and damage to those assets; in turn, the resulting climate adaptations are concentrated on changes to physical infrastructure, such as hardening or relocating facilities, which can be inherently difficult or expensive. Applying the functional lens suggested by the NCF framework not only allows communities to have a more comprehensive understanding of how climate risk could manifest and helps them identify and prioritize which functions are most necessary to sustain a community but also expands the potential set of climate adaptation strategies.

For example, the use of the NCF framework suggests adaptation measures related primarily to changing the underlying demand for a function (e.g., adaptation by individual property owners) or addressing considerations related to the workforce that provides it (e.g., national volunteer auxiliaries). This more comprehensive focus provides additional options for mitigating risk to the most-basic and -essential functions of a community while considering but not being limited to the physical assets associated with their provision.

Additionally, the NCF structure facilitates consideration of the functional relationships (interdependencies) among NCFs, which describe how risk can propagate through the system. These sources of risk must also be mitigated, but, in some cases, the actors that mitigate these risks are only a subset of those stakeholders that could benefit from the activity.

A comprehensive understanding of an NCF's risk profile is crucial for developing effective mitigation strategies, yet **there are not always sufficient data across these NCFs to provide insight into specific system risks or for specific localities**. Additional data on NCF functional and geospatial relationships could support a more complete understanding of an NCF's risk profile and help better prioritize investments in risk mitigation. For example, lack of transparency across a supply chain makes *Maintain Supply Chains* vulnerable to extended disruptions. Incorporating data, such as those provided through blockchain technology, into a supply chain reduces risk because it provides a set of data about all links in a supply chain that any of the users can access. This visibility mitigates risk by allowing users to gain information quickly about the location of goods, as well as where they have been and where they are being shipped. For *Provide Insurance Services*, improvements in public data on infrastructure and climate hazards would support better forecasts of climate change risk, which are fundamental to actuarial modeling and pricing decisions for insurance, as well as for understanding the value of different mitigation strategies.

Understanding how an NCF is provided and who provides it is crucial for identifying options for risk mitigation. The manner in which an NCF is provided and who provides it have major implications for how—and how feasible—it might be to mitigate risk to the NCF. For example, we examined two NCFs, *Prepare for and Manage Emergencies* and *Provide Public Safety*, that are provided predominantly at the local level by a large number of distributed entities. This has significant implications for risk mitigation because it suggests that solutions need to be focused either on enhancing the capabilities of a very large number of providers, many of which might be small and resource constrained, or on addressing the net overall demand for the NCF. For example, providing local jurisdictions free access to communication technologies and training on how to use them could reduce response times and limit disruptions, but insufficient staff capacity to adopt new technologies and undertake training reduces the widespread feasibility of this strategy. In contrast, other NCFs, such as *Maintain Supply Chains*, are distributed across a broad array of actors in both the public and private sectors and of varying sizes and capabilities. In those cases, not all mitigation strategies might be relevant to all actors, and determining how individual incremental investments in strategies that make sense from a given actor's perspective contribute to overall risk mitigation for the NCF will be complicated. For example, relying on strategic stockpiles of critical goods is not necessarily straightforward because the balance between the needed amounts and the cost of maintaining stockpiles varies widely across supply chains and the products and firms within them.

The NCFs assessed for this report might be representative of other NCFs and thereby suggest the likely range and quality of mitigation strategies available to other NCFs. For example, we found a relatively limited number of options for *Provide Public Safety*; this fact could be largely a function of the manner in which the NCF is provided and how it interacts with climate change. Although they are not directly analogous, other NCFs, such as *Enforce Law* and *Provide Medical Care*, might be structured similarly to *Provide Public Safety*, which implies that the number of options to mitigate risk to those NCFs might be similar to that for *Provide Public Safety* (and, potentially, similarly constrained).

In some cases, it appears that **mitigating indirect risk to an NCF might be as effective as (or more effective than) mitigating direct risk to the NCF itself**. For example, although direct risk from climate change is a significant source of risk to *Provide Public Safety*, this NCF is also at considerable cascading risk from climate change–related disruption to other NCFs, such as *Distribute Electricity*. Here is one illustration: Hurricanes Irma and Maria damaged Puerto Rico's entire energy grid, which resulted in cascading disruptions to transportation, communications, water supply, stormwater management, hospitals, key archival storage facilities, and wastewater treatment facilities.[1] Given the limited options to mitigate direct risk from climate change to *Provide Public Safety* and the importance of *Distribute Electricity* to it and to a large number of other NCFs, a more effective use of resources might be to attempt to mitigate risk to *Distribute Electricity*. This scenario is likely to apply to multiple NCFs and suggests that a broader variety of entities might be able to reduce risk to any given NCF and that more-diverse policy options might be available than might initially appear to be the case given the structure of the NCF.

The experience developing a recovery plan for Puerto Rico also provides an illustrative example of how climate adaptation priority-setting might occur for one or more NCFs. During Puerto Rico's recovery planning process, priorities were set for recovery actions holistically by grouping recovery actions developed from a bottom-up determination of damage and needs into a different portfolio for each sector. The portfolios addressed Puerto Rico's recovery objectives and strategic priorities, but each emphasized different goals. For example, one might emphasize the lowest cost, while another might emphasize resilient recovery. Interdependencies were addressed through cross-sector stakeholder communication and planning. Because of these interdependencies, most portfolios include actions from multiple sectors. Decisionmakers chose from the portfolios options to include in the plan with the aid of a decision support tool that arrayed basic information about cost, objectives addressed, and general effectiveness of the portfolios for meeting recovery goals.[2] NCF interdependence remains a critical issue to assess, but this is one example of an approach that could be used to prioritize climate risk adaptation strategies for implementation.

Similarly, **coordinated efforts targeting priority climate risks might be more impactful in reducing risks than siloed activities would be**. Because each NCF has multiple actors with their own roles, responsibilities, and priorities, current risk mitigation activities are often diffuse and uncoordinated. One option moving forward might be for certain entities, such as CISA or other federal actors, to play an important role in convening or facilitating such coordination among regional, state, or local governments and nonprofits. For example, the Southeast Florida Regional Climate Change Compact, which is a voluntary collaborative effort by Broward, Miami-Dade, Monroe, and Palm Beach counties to improve climate mitigation and adaptation planning and coordination in the region, provides a platform for

> engaging state and federal agencies and educating the public on policy issues important to the region, pursuing funding for climate resilience, developing regionally consistent planning assumptions derived from scientific analyses, providing needed information and technical guidance to local governments to improve climate resilience, and identifying issues of mutual concern that are better served through a coordinated response. This

---

[1] Fischbach et al., *After Hurricane Maria*.

[2] Burger et al., *Developing Recovery Options for Puerto Rico's Economic and Disaster Recovery Plan*.

platform can be used to steer work with regional, municipal, nonprofit, academic, and private sector organizations.[3]

Through the compact, members have been able to attract investment from outside sources, reduce duplication of effort, affect Florida planning legislation, facilitate climate adaptation by cities and counties in the region, and develop adaptation strategies and assessment tools.

Furthermore, to understand how climate risk can be mitigated holistically, it is important to focus on broader issues of policy and systemic vulnerabilities, including cascading effects from other NCFs. No NCF exists in a vacuum, and mitigating risk means dealing with political and societal issues. Some solutions might be most effective when implemented at federal scales or require a portfolio approach to address systemic risks or avoid maladaptation.[4] For example, for *Provide Insurance Services*, both insurers and state and local governments can deploy strategies that support the actions of property owners and their communities and mitigate the consequences of climate change to insurance markets overall. However, the effectiveness of risk mitigation efforts depends on people's risk behavior and their willingness to invest in risk reduction for their own properties. Although these political, societal, and other systemic issues can complicate risk management and make transformational change more difficult, risk mitigation focused on the short term or on incremental change can still be viable and is also important.

Future Work

In this report, we have presented information on strategies that could mitigate the more-significant risks that climate change poses to an NCF, enablers of these strategies, and barriers to their implementation. Because climate change adaptation could involve multiple actors and stakeholders, as well as uncertainty about climate drivers and the effectiveness of risk mitigations, future work could extend the analysis of the strategies presented in this report to provide practical guidance and information to entities that are starting to plan for and implement their own mitigation-related investments. Practical guidance could be developed from case studies of additional climate adaptation strategies already in place to identify the lessons learned from those actors that have implemented them, such as how enablers were leveraged and barriers overcome, how to measure how well an investment reduced risk or increased resilience, or whether there were cobenefits or unintended consequences.

Further work could also be done to describe how strategies could be adapted to changing climate conditions as a part of an adaptive management approach to climate risk mitigation.

---

[3] Resetar et al., *Guidebook for Multi-Agency Collaboration for Sustainability and Resilience*, p. 60.

[4] Maladaptation occurs when a strategy decreases vulnerability to climate change impacts in the short term but either intentionally or unintentionally increases vulnerability in the long term. This can occur when a strategy exacerbates existing disparities or vulnerabilities, shifts vulnerability, or creates new vulnerabilities.

Importantly, robust risk management does not end with identifying and mitigating risk but includes monitoring risk reduction and tracking changes in the risk landscape. In this vein, future work to support NCF actors in risk mitigation could also involve methods for understanding and tracking progress toward effectively mitigating climate risk from particular climate drivers and identifying additional opportunities for adjusting existing strategies to the changing risk landscape.

We focused on four high-priority NCFs. However, there is much to be learned by performing a similar analysis for the other 51 NCFs, particularly NCFs that are highly interconnected with, and depended on by, a large number of other NCFs or those at high risk of disruption due to climate change. Similarly, tools to conduct interdependence analysis would provide additional context about the return on investment not only within an NCF from adopting a specific climate adaptation strategy but also across NCFs. It is not unreasonable to expect that mitigating risk to a highly interconnected NCF, even if doing so is expensive, could reduce risk across a large number of NCFs, making such a strategy a far better, and more important, investment than it might appear when assessed for a single NCF.

Another line of future work that would be useful to entities that own NCFs is tools to provide decision support to help select between and prioritize among alternative climate adaptation measures. These tools could consider a variety of aspects of adaptation measures. For example, enhanced tools could help conduct cost–benefit analyses to identify which adaptation measures are likely to provide the greatest returns on investment while limiting the potential for maladaptation. Climate adaptation measures that address nonphysical aspects of critical infrastructure, such as changing demand for an NCF, might ultimately be more cost-effective than physical adaptations. However, the relative cost-effectiveness of various adaptation measures might be very difficult to determine given the lack of information currently available about the costs and benefits of various strategies.

Abbreviations

CISA	Cybersecurity and Infrastructure Security Agency
COVID-19	coronavirus disease 2019
DOT	U.S. Department of Transportation
EMS	emergency medical services
ESG	environmental, social, and governance
FAIR	fair access to insurance requirements
FEMA	Federal Emergency Management Agency
IAIS	International Association of Insurance Supervisors
IBHS	Insurance Institute for Business and Home Safety
MOA	memorandum of agreement
MOU	memorandum of understanding
NACo	National Association of Counties
NAIC	National Association of Insurance Commissioners
NCF	National Critical Function
PPE	personal protective equipment
SLTT	state, local, tribal, or territorial
SNS	Strategic National Stockpile
TCFD	Task Force on Climate-Related Financial Disclosures

Bibliography

Abbott, Chris, "An Uncertain Future: Law Enforcement, National Security and Climate Change," briefing paper, Oxford Research Group, January 2008.

AECOM, *Port of Los Angeles: Sea Level Rise Adaptation Study—Final Draft*, prepared for Port of Los Angeles, September 2018.

Allen, Thomas R., George McLeod, and Sheila Hutt, "Sea Level Rise Exposure Assessment of U.S. East Coast Cargo Container Terminals," *Maritime Policy and Management*, Vol. 49, No. 4, 2022.

Allison-Aipa, Timothy S., Gabriel M. De La Rosa, Melba C. Stetz, and Carl A. Castro, "The Impact of National Guard Activation for Homeland Defense: Employers' Perspective," *Military Medicine*, Vol. 170, No. 10, October 2005.

Amacher, Ezra, "FEMA Hit by Multi-State Lawsuit over Flood Insurance Rating Formula," *Insurance Journal*, June 2, 2023.

American Association of Port Authorities, "Port Planning and Investment Toolkit," webpage, undated. As of October 23, 2023:
https://www.aapa-ports.org/empowering/content.aspx?ItemNumber=21263

Angel, Jim, Chris Swanston, Barbara Mayes Boustead, Kathryn C. Conlon, Kimberly R. Hall, Jenna L. Jorns, Kenneth E. Kunkel, Maria Carmen Lemos, Brent Lofgren, Todd A. Ontl, John Posey, Kim Stone, Eugene Takle, and Dennis Todey, "Midwest," in David Reidmiller, Christopher W. Avery, David R. Easterling, Kenneth E. Kunkel, Kristin Lewis, Thomas K. Maycock, and Brooke C. Stewart, eds., *Impacts, Risks, and Adaptation in the United States: Fourth National Climate Assessment*, Vol. II, U.S. Global Change Research Program, 2018.

Archer, Megan, Katherine Pedersen, Mallory Kennedy, and Nicole A. Errett, "Integrating Health Considerations into Local Level Recovery Planning: An Exploration of Florida's Recovery and Redevelopment Plans," *Journal of Disaster Research*, Vol. 17, No. 7, 2022.

Austin, Nick, "Excessive Heat Can Impact Rails as Well as Driver Health," *FreightWaves*, July 8, 2019.

Baker, John S., Jr., "State Police Powers and the Federalization of Local Crime," *Temple Law Review*, Vol. 72, No. 3, Fall 1999.

Baker, Katie, "Climate Change Will Offer Long-Term Tailwinds: Goldman Sachs," *Reinsurance News*, February 4, 2022.

Barnosky, Jason Thomas, Andrew Lauland, Michelle E. Miro, Jay Balagna, Liisa Ecola, Soo Kim, Chelsea Kolb, Kristin J. Leuschner, Ian Mitch, Andrew M. Parker, Leslie Adrienne Payne, Carter C. Price, Tucker Reese, Liam Regan, Susan A. Resetar, Christopher M. Schnaubelt, Rachel Steratore, and Karen M. Sudkamp, *Streamlining Emergency Management: Issues, Impacts, and Options for Improvement*, Homeland Security Operational Analysis Center operated by the RAND Corporation, RR-A1440-5, 2022. As of May 5, 2023:
https://www.rand.org/pubs/research_reports/RRA1440-5.html

Bathgate, Kyle, Jingran Sun, Shidong Pan, Srijith Balakrishnan, Zhanmin Zhang, Michael Murphy, Zhe Han, and Lisa Loftus-Otway, *Creating a Resilient Port System in Texas: Assessing and Mitigating Extreme Weather Events—Final Report*, Center for Transportation Research, University of Texas at Austin, May 1, 2022.

Benevolenza, Mia A., and LeaAnne DeRigne, "The Impact of Climate Change and Natural Disasters on Vulnerable Populations: A Systematic Review of Literature," *Journal of Human Behavior in the Social Environment*, Vol. 29, No. 2, 2019.

Berke, Philip, John Cooper, Meghan Aminto, Shannon Grabich, and Jennifer Horney, "Adaptive Planning for Disaster Recovery and Resiliency: An Evaluation of 87 Local Recovery Plans in Eight States," *Journal of the American Planning Association*, Vol. 80, No. 4, 2014.

Berman v. Parker, 348 U.S. 26, November 22, 1954.

Bevere, Lucia, and Andreas Weigel, "Natural Catastrophes in 2020: Secondary Perils in the Spotlight, but Don't Forget Primary-Peril Risks," Sigma 1/2021, March 30, 2021.

"Blockchain's Disconnect Between the Could-Be and the Has-Been," *FreightWaves*, February 15, 2019.

Bolinger, Rebecca A., Vincent M. Brown, Christopher M. Fuhrmann, Karin L. Gleason, T. Andrew Joyner, Barry D. Keim, Amanda Lewis, John W. Nielsen-Gammon, Crystal J. Stiles, William Tollefson, Hannah E. Attard, and Alicia M. Bentley, "An Assessment of the Extremes and Impacts of the February 2021 South-Central U.S. Arctic Outbreak, and How Climate Services Can Help," *Weather and Climate Extremes*, Vol. 36, June 2022.

Born, Patricia, and Robert Klein, *Best Practices for Regulating Property Insurance Premiums and Managing Natural Catastrophe Risk in the United States*, National Association of Mutual Insurance Companies, November 2015.

Boston Planning and Development Agency, "Coastal Flood Resilience Guidelines and Zoning Overlay District (Article 25A)," webpage, undated. As of May 18, 2023:
https://www.bostonplans.org/planning/planning-initiatives/
flood-resiliency-building-guidelines-zoning-over

Bourtembourg, Jérôme, Laura Languedoc, George Overton, and Marcelo Ramella, *The Impact of Climate Change on the Financial Stability of the Insurance Sector*, International Association of Insurance Supervisors, Global Insurance Market Report, 2021.

Buchanan, Paula R., and Chayne Sparagowski, "The Role of Emerging Technologies and Social Justice in Emergency Management Practice: The Good, the Bad, and the Future," in Alessandra Jerolleman and William L. Waugh, Jr., eds., *Justice, Equity, and Emergency Management*, Vol. 25, Emerald Publishing Limited, 2022.

Bundy, Sarah J., and Jessica Jensen, "The Role of the County-Elected Official in Disaster Recovery," *Risk, Hazards, and Crisis in Public Policy*, Vol. 6, No. 3, September 2015.

Burger, Nicholas E., Cynthia R. Cook, Melissa L. Finucane, David G. Groves, Justin Hannah Hodiak, Anu Narayanan, Karishma V. Patel, Lara Schmidt, Aaron Strong, and Katie Whipkey, *Developing Recovery Options for Puerto Rico's Economic and Disaster Recovery Plan: Process and Methodology*, Homeland Security Operational Analysis Center operated by the RAND Corporation, RR-2597-DHS, 2020. As of October 21, 2023:
https://www.rand.org/pubs/research_reports/RR2597.html

Cachon, Gerard P., Santiago Gallino, and Marcelo Olivares, "Severe Weather and Automobile Assembly Productivity," Columbia Business School, Research Paper 12/37, last revised December 22, 2012.

California Department of Insurance, "Mandatory One Year Moratorium on Non-Renewals," webpage, undated. As of December 15, 2023:
https://www.insurance.ca.gov/01-consumers/140-catastrophes/
MandatoryOneYearMoratoriumNonRenewals.cfm

Calma, Justine, "Texas' Natural Gas Production Just Froze Under Pressure," *The Verge*, February 17, 2021.

Center for Insurance Policy and Research, National Association of Insurance Commissioners, "Fair Access to Insurance Requirements (FAIR) Plans," last updated February 1, 2023.

Central Manpower Base, Singapore Ministry of Defence, "Discover NS," webpage, undated. As of May 10, 2023:
https://www.cmpb.gov.sg/web/portal/cmpb/home/about-us/discover-ns

Chang, Kuo-Liang, "A Reliable Waterway System Is Important to Agriculture," U.S. Department of Agriculture, Agriculture Marketing Service, February 2022.

Chicago Region Environmental and Transportation Efficiency Program, "About CREATE," webpage, undated. As of May 18, 2023:
https://www.createprogram.org/about-create/history/

Chicago Region Environmental and Transportation Efficiency Program, "2023 Newsletter," April 2023.

Chopra, Sunil, and ManMohan S. Sodhi, "Reducing the Risk of Supply Chain Disruptions," *MIT Sloan Management Review*, March 18, 2014.

CISA—*See* Cybersecurity and Infrastructure Security Agency.

Clancy, Noreen, Melissa L. Finucane, Jordan R. Fischbach, David G. Groves, Debra Knopman, Karishma V. Patel, and Lloyd Dixon, *The Building Resilient Infrastructure and Communities Mitigation Grant Program: Incorporating Hazard Risk and Social Equity into Decisionmaking Processes*, Homeland Security Operational Analysis Center operated by the RAND Corporation, RR-A1258-1, 2022. As of May 1, 2023:
https://www.rand.org/pubs/research_reports/RRA1258-1.html

Collier, Stephen J., Rebecca Elliott, and Turo-Kimmo Lehtonen, "Climate Change and Insurance," *Economy and Society*, Vol. 50, No. 2, 2021.

Committee on Science, Engineering, and Public Policy and Committee on Increasing National Resilience to Hazards and Disasters, National Research Council, *Disaster Resilience: A National Imperative*, National Academies Press, 2012.

Congressional Research Service, "Amdt10.3.2 State Police Power and Tenth Amendment Jurisprudence," *Constitution Annotated*, webpage, undated. As of May 10, 2023:
https://constitution.congress.gov/browse/essay/amdt10-3-2/ALDE_00013622/

Cooper, John T., "Reflections on Engaging Socially Vulnerable Populations in Disaster Planning," in Michael Lindell, ed., *The Routledge Handbook of Urban Disaster Resilience*, Routledge, 2019.

Council on Environmental Quality, Executive Office of the President, "Environmental Impact Statement Timelines (2010–2018)," White House, June 12, 2020.

Craig, Robin Kundis, "Coastal Adaptation, Government-Subsidized Insurance, and Perverse Incentives to Stay," *Climatic Change*, Vol. 152, January 30, 2019.

Currie, Chris P., director, Homeland Security and Justice, U.S. Governmental Accountability Office, *FEMA Workforce: Long-Standing and New Challenges Could Affect Mission Success*, testimony before the U.S. House of Representatives Committee on Homeland Security Subcommittee on Emergency Preparedness, Response, and Recovery and Subcommittee on Oversight, Management, and Accountability, GAO-22-105631, January 20, 2022.

Cybersecurity and Infrastructure Security Agency, U.S. Department of Homeland Security, "National Critical Functions," webpage, undated. As of October 23, 2023: https://www.cisa.gov/topics/risk-management/national-critical-functions

Cybersecurity and Infrastructure Security Agency, U.S. Department of Homeland Security, "National Critical Functions: Status Update to the Critical Infrastructure Community," July 2020.

da Cruz, Nuno F., Philipp Rode, and Michael McQuarrie, "New Urban Governance: A Review of Current Themes and Future Priorities," *Journal of Urban Affairs*, Vol. 41, No. 1, 2019.

Deloitte Center for Financial Services, "Climate Risk: Regulators Sharpen Their Focus—Helping Insurers Navigate the Climate Risk Landscape," 2019.

Deubelli, Teresa Maria, and Reinhard Mechler, "Perspectives on Transformational Change in Climate Risk Management and Adaptation," *Environmental Research Letters*, Vol. 16, No. 5, April 27, 2021.

Digital Container Shipping Association, homepage, undated. As of October 23, 2023: https://dcsa.org

Dixon, Lloyd, Flavia Tsang, and Gary Fitts, "California Wildfires: Can Insurance Markets Handle the Risk?" RAND Corporation, RB-A635-1, 2020. As of October 11, 2022: https://www.rand.org/pubs/research_briefs/RBA635-1.html

Dong, Jing, Micah Makaiwi, Navid Shafieirad, and Yundi Huang, *Modeling Multimodal Freight Transportation Network Performance Under Disruptions: Final Report*, Center for Transportation Research and Education, Iowa State University, MATC-ISU 237, 2015.

DOT—*See* U.S. Department of Transportation.

Dzigbede, Komla D., Sarah Beth Gehl, and Katherine Willoughby, "Disaster Resiliency of U.S. Local Governments: Insights to Strengthen Local Response and Recovery from the COVID-19 Pandemic," *Public Administration Review*, Vol. 8, No. 4, July–August 2020.

Easterling, David R., Kenneth E. Kunkel, J. R. Arnold, T. Knutson, Allegra N. LeGrande, L. R. Leung, Russell S. Vose, Duane E. Waliser, and Michael F. Wehner, "Precipitation Change in the United States," in Donald J. Wuebbles, David W. Fahey, Kathy A. Hibbard, David J. Dokken, Brooke C. Stewart, and Thomas K. Maycock, eds., *Climate Science Special Report: Fourth National Climate Assessment*, Vol. I, U.S. Global Change Research Program, 2017.

Ecola, Liisa, Aaron C. Davenport, Kenneth Kuhn, Alexander D. Rothenberg, Eric Cooper, Mark Barrett, Thomas F. Atkin, and Jeffrey Kendall, *Rebuilding Surface, Maritime, and Air Transportation in Puerto Rico After Hurricanes Irma and Maria: Supporting Documentation for the Puerto Rico Recovery Plan*, Homeland Security Operational Analysis Center operated by the RAND Corporation, RR-2607-DHS, 2020. As of May 18, 2023: https://www.rand.org/pubs/research_reports/RR2607.html

Egan, Matthew Jude, and Gabor H. Tischler, "The National Voluntary Organizations Active in Disaster Relief and Disaster Assistance Missions: An Approach to Better Collaboration with the Public Sector in Post-Disaster Operations," *Risk, Hazards, and Crisis in Public Policy*, Vol. 1, No. 2, July 2010.

Eichorn, Abigail, *Qualitative Exploratory Case Study: The Generation Gap in Emergency Management in the Six State Area Covered by FEMA's Region 8*, doctoral dissertation, Colorado Technical University, May 2021.

Eller, Warren S., and Brian J. Gerber, *Voluntary Nonprofit Organizations and Disaster Recovery: Assessing the Value of the Nonprofit Contributions to the 2009 Alaskan Rivers Flood Recovery Effort*, report prepared for National Voluntary Organizations Active in Disaster, 2010.

Emergency Management Higher Education Project, Federal Emergency Management Agency, U.S. Department of Homeland Security, "Principles of Emergency Management Supplement," September 11, 2007.

Environmental Resilience Institute, "Strategies for Climate Change Adaptation," webpage, undated. As of December 15, 2023:
https://eri.iu.edu/erit/strategies/index.html

Ergun, Ozlem, Wallace J. Hopp, and Pinar Keskinocak, "A Structured Overview of Insights and Opportunities for Enhancing Supply Chain Resilience," *IISE Transactions*, Vol. 55, No. 1, 2023.

Ernst, Sean, Daphne LaDue, and Alan Gerard, "Understanding Emergency Manager Forecast Use in Severe Weather Events," *Journal of Operational Meteorology*, Vol. 6, No. 9, 2018.

Fagan, Kevin, Natalie Ambrosio Preudhomme, and Caglar Demir, *Insurance Costs Trends Becoming a Headache for the CRE Market*, Moody's Analytics, August 3, 2023.

Federal Emergency Management Agency, U.S. Department of Homeland Security, *Pre-Disaster Recovery Planning Guide for Local Governments*, FD 008-03, February 2017.

Federal Emergency Management Agency, U.S. Department of Homeland Security, "Mission Areas and Core Capabilities," webpage, last updated July 20, 2020. As of October 4, 2022:
https://www.fema.gov/emergency-managers/national-preparedness/mission-core-capabilities

Federal Permitting Improvement Steering Council, "Federal Permitting Improvement Steering Council (FPISC) Agencies," webpage, last updated August 28, 2019. As of May 18, 2023:
https://www.permits.performance.gov/about/
federal-permitting-improvement-steering-council-fpisc-agencies

FEMA—*See* Federal Emergency Management Agency.

Fischbach, Jordan R., Linnea Warren May, Katie Whipkey, Shoshana R. Shelton, Christine Anne Vaughan, Devin Tierney, Kristin J. Leuschner, Lisa S. Meredith, and Hilary J. Peterson, *After Hurricane Maria: Predisaster Conditions, Hurricane Damage, and Recovery Needs in Puerto Rico*, Homeland Security Operational Analysis Center operated by the RAND Corporation, RR-2595-DHS, 2020. As of October 22, 2023:
https://www.rand.org/pubs/research_reports/RR2595.html

Fredman, Alex, "Regulators Should Identify and Mitigate Climate Risks in the Insurance Industry," Center for American Progress, June 13, 2022.

Fremont-Smith, Marion, Elizabeth T. Boris, and C. Eugene Steuerle, "Charities' Response to Disasters: Expectations and Realities," in Elizabeth T. Boris and C. Eugene Steuerle, eds., *After Katrina: Public Expectation and Charities' Response*, Urban Institute, May 2006.

Gazzale, Laurie, "Motivational Implications Leading to the Continued Commitment of Volunteer Firefighters," *International Journal of Emergency Services*, Vol. 8, No. 2, 2019.

Georgetown Climate Center, Georgetown Law School, "Managed Retreat Toolkit," webpage, undated. As of October 23, 2023:
https://www.georgetownclimate.org/adaptation/toolkits/managed-retreat-toolkit/
introduction.html

Gershon, Robyn R., Michelle A. Muska, Qi Zhi, and Lewis E. Kraus, "Are Local Offices of Emergency Management Prepared for People with Disabilities? Results from the FEMA Region 9 Survey," *Journal of Emergency Management*, Vol. 19, No. 1, January–February 2021.

Gnanarajah, Raj, and Gary Shorter, "Introduction to Financial Services: Environmental, Social, and Governance (ESG) Issues," Congressional Research Service, IF11716, updated January 5, 2023.

Goin, Dana E., Kara E. Rudolph, and Jennifer Ahern, "Impact of Drought on Crime in California: A Synthetic Control Approach," *PLoS ONE*, Vol. 12, No. 10, 2017.

Goodman, J. David, "Amazon Pulls Out of Planned New York City Headquarters," *New York Times*, February 14, 2019.

Grimaldi, Antonio, Kia Javanmardian, Dickon Pinner, Hamid Samandari, and Kurt Strovink, "Climate Change and P&C Insurance: The Threat and Opportunity," McKinsey and Company, November 19, 2020.

Groshong, Lisa, Jeffrey Czajkowski, Paula Harms, Juan Zhang, and Miranda Dahman, *Assessment of and Insights from NAIC Climate Risk Disclosure Data*, Center for Insurance Policy and Research, National Association of Insurance Commissioners, November 2020.

Hartwig, Robert P., and Claire Wilkinson, *Residual Market Property Plans: From Markets of Last Resort to Markets of First Choice*, Insurance Information Institute, May 2016.

Helper, Susan, and Evan Soltas, "Why the Pandemic Has Disrupted Supply Chains," Council of Economic Advisers, White House, June 17, 2021.

Herweijer, Celine, Nicola Ranger, and Robert E. T. Ward, "Adaptation to Climate Change: Threats and Opportunities for the Insurance Industry," *Geneva Papers on Risk and Insurance: Issues and Practice*, Vol. 34, July 1, 2009.

Hippe, Ariel, Austin Becker, Martin Fischer, and Benedict Schwegler, *Estimation of Cost Required to Elevate US Ports in Response to Climate Change: A Thought Exercise for Climate Critical Resources*, Stanford University, Civil and Environmental Engineering Department, Center for Integrated Facility Engineering, Working Paper WP138, December 2015.

Hirtzer, Michael, Elizabeth Elkin, and Joe Deaux, "Dwindling Mississippi Grounds Barges, Threatens Shipments," Bloomberg, October 5, 2022.

Horn, Diane P., "National Flood Insurance Program Risk Rating 2.0: Frequently Asked Questions," Congressional Research Service, IN11777, version 6, updated May 1, 2023.

Horney, Jennifer A., Ashley I. Naimi, Ward Lyles, Matt Simon, David Salvesen, and Philip Berke, "Assessing the Relationship Between Hazard Mitigation Plan Quality and Rural Status in a Cohort of 57 Counties from 3 States in the Southeastern U.S.," *Challenges*, Vol. 3, 2012.

Horney, Jennifer, Mai Nguyen, David Salvesen, Caroline Dwyer, John Cooper, and Philip Berke, "Assessing the Quality of Rural Hazard Mitigation Plans in the Southeastern United States," *Journal of Planning Education and Research*, Vol. 7, No. 1, March 2017.

Hu, Patricia S., Rolf R. Schmitt, Ramond Robinson, Matthew Chambers, William H. Moore, and Alpha Wingfield, *2023 Port Performance Freight Statistics Program: Annual Report to Congress*, Bureau of Transportation Statistics, Office of the Secretary of Transportation, U.S. Department of Transportation, January 2023.

IAIS—*See* International Association of Insurance Supervisors.

IBHS—*See* Insurance Institute for Business and Home Safety.

Insurance Information Institute, "Residual Markets," *A Firm Foundation: How Insurance Supports the Economy*, undated.

Insurance Institute for Business and Home Safety, "Financial Incentives," webpage, undated. As of May 14, 2023:
https://fortifiedhome.org/incentives/

International Air Transportation Association, "What Types of Cargo Are Transported by Air?" September 7, 2022.

International Association of Insurance Supervisors, *Application Paper on the Supervision of Climate-Related Risks in the Insurance Sector*, May 2021.

International City/County Management Association, "Disaster Resilience and Recovery Survey: Summary of Survey Results," December 2019.

Interstate Commission for EMS Personnel Practice, "What Is the EMS Compact?" webpage, undated. As of May 10, 2023:
https://www.emscompact.gov/the-compact/what-is-the-ems-compact

Jennings, Eliot, Sudha Arlikatti, and Simon Andrew, "Determinants of Emergency Management Decision Support Software Technology: An Empirical Analysis of Social Influence in Technology Adoption," *Journal of Homeland Security and Emergency Management*, Vol. 12, No. 3, 2015.

Jensen, Jessica, Sarah Bundy, Brian Thomas, and Mariama Yakubu, "The County Emergency Manager's Role in Disaster Recovery," *International Journal of Mass Emergencies and Disasters*, Vol. 32, No. 1, March 2014.

Jensen, Jessica, and Marcelo Ferreira, "An Exploration of Local Emergency Management Program Accreditation Pursuit," *Journal of Homeland Security and Emergency Management*, Vol. 20, No. 3, September 2023.

Jensen, Jessica, and Sarah J. Bundy Kirkpatrick, "Local Recovery Coordinators and the National Disaster Recovery Framework: Questions Regarding the Form, Necessity, and Potential of the Role," *Journal of Homeland Security and Emergency Management*, Vol. 14, 2017.

Jensen, Jessica, and Sarah Kirkpatrick, "Local Emergency Management and Comprehensive Emergency Management (CEM): A Discussion Prompted by Interviews with Chief Resilience Officers," *International Journal of Disaster Risk Reduction*, Vol. 79, September 2022.

Kahn, Matthew E., Brian Casey, and Nolan Jones, "How the Insurance Industry Can Push Us to Prepare for Climate Change," *Harvard Business Review*, August 28, 2017.

Kanell, Michael E., and Greg Bluestein, "Expansion of GA Ports Pays Dividends to Economy, Companies, Jobs," *Atlanta Journal-Constitution*, April 15, 2022.

Kang, Seong C., "Volunteer Involvement and Organizational Performance: The Use of Volunteer Officers in Public Safety," *Public Performance and Management Review*, Vol. 42, No. 3, 2019.

Kapucu, Naim, and Qian Hu, "Understanding Multiplexity of Collaborative Emergency Management Networks," *American Review of Public Administration*, Vol. 46, No. 4, July 2016.

Keenan, Robert A., "The Shortfall of Qualified Applicants and the Generational Implications That Impact Law Enforcement," leadership white paper submitted in partial fulfillment of a requirement to graduate from the Leadership Command College, Bill Blackwood Law Enforcement Management Institute of Texas, February 2017.

Kincaid, Erika, "Is Grocery Store Salmon Really Wild? Blockchain Has the Answer," *Food Dive*, January 4, 2018.

Kintziger, Kristina W., Kahler W. Stone, Meredith A. Jagger, and Jennifer A. Horney, "The Impact of the COVID-19 Response on the Provision of Other Public Health Services in the U.S.: A Cross Sectional Study," *PLoS ONE*, Vol. 16, No. 10, 2021.

Kobziar, Leda N., and George R. Thompson III, "Wildfire Smoke, a Potential Infectious Agent," *Science*, Vol. 370, No. 6523, December 18, 2020.

Kossin, J. P., T. Hall, T. Knutson, Kenneth E. Kunkel, Robert J. Trapp, Duane E. Waliser, and Michael F. Wehner, "Extreme Storms," in Donald J. Wuebbles, David W. Fahey, Kathy A. Hibbard, David J. Dokken, Brooke C. Stewart, and Thomas K. Maycock, eds., *Climate Science Special Report: Fourth National Climate Assessment*, Vol. I, U.S. Global Change Research Program, 2017. As of November 6, 2022:
https://www.doi.org/10.7930/J07S7KXX

Kulken, Todd, and Frank Gottron, "The Strategic National Stockpile: Overview and Issues for Congress," Congressional Research Service, R47400, updated September 26, 2023.

Kunreuther, Howard C., and Erwann O. Michel-Kerjan, *Climate Change, Insurability of Large-Scale Disasters and the Emerging Liability Challenge*, National Bureau of Economic Research, Working Paper 12821, January 2007.

Kunreuther, Howard, Erwann Michel-Kerjan, and Nicola Ranger, "Insuring Future Climate Catastrophes," *Climatic Change*, Vol. 118, May 2013.

Lachman, Beth E., R. J. Briggs, Michael T. Wilson, Susan A. Resetar, Jon Niewijk, and Philip Song, *Valuing Army Installation Resilience Investments for Natural Hazards: Exploring the Use of Insurance Methods and Historical Installation Storm Damage*, RAND Corporation, RR-A2382-1, 2023. As of December 12, 2023:
https://www.rand.org/pubs/research_reports/RRA2382-1.html

Lantz, Emelie, and Marcus Runefors, "Recruitment, Retention and Resignation Among Non-Career Firefighters," *International Journal of Emergency Services*, Vol. 10, No. 1, 2021.

LaRocco, Lori Ann, "New York Is Now the Nation's Busiest Port in a Historic Tipping Point for U.S.-Bound Trade," CNBC, updated September 24, 2022.

Lauland, Andrew, Liam Regan, Susan A. Resetar, Joie D. Acosta, Rahim Ali, Edward W. Chan, Richard H. Donohue, Liisa Ecola, Timothy R. Gulden, Chelsea Kolb, Kristin J. Leuschner, Tobias Sytsma, Patricia A. Stapleton, Michael T. Wilson, and Chandler Sachs, *Strategies to Mitigate the Risk to the National Critical Functions Generated by Climate Change*, Homeland Security Operational Analysis Center operated by the RAND Corporation, RR-A1645-1, 2023. As of December 12, 2023:
https://www.rand.org/pubs/research_reports/RRA1645-1.html

Lawrence, Robyn Griggs, "How Contractors Use Tech to Tighten Up Supply Chains," *Supply Chain Dive*, April 26, 2023.

Leibovici, Fernando, and Jason Dunn, "Supply Chain Bottlenecks and Inflation: The Role of Semiconductors," *Economic Synopses*, No. 28, 2021.

Leonard, Matt, "As Storms Become More Frequent and Volatile, Some Ports Plan for the Risk—but Most Do Not," *Trucking Dive*, June 1, 2021.

Littlejohn, Mann and Associates, *Seaports Resiliency Report*, Florida Seaport Transportation and Economic Development Council, 2019.

Liu, Fang, Jing-Sheng Song, and Jordan D. Tong, "Building Supply Chain Resilience Through Virtual Stockpile Pooling," *Production and Operations Management*, Vol. 25, No. 10, October 2016.

Lockridge, Deborah, "Blockchain, Once Overhyped, Is Finding Real Transportation Use Cases," *Truckinginfo*, October 12, 2022.

Los Angeles County Public Works, "Public Works Volunteer Program," webpage, undated. As of May 10, 2023:
https://pw.lacounty.gov/volunteer/

MacKenzie, Ellen J., and Anthony R. Carlini, *Characterizing Local EMS Systems*, U.S. Department of Transportation, National Highway Traffic Safety Administration, DOT HS 811 824, August 2013.

Madrigano, Jaime, Anita Chandra, Tracy Costigan, and Joie D. Acosta, "Beyond Disaster Preparedness: Building a Resilience-Oriented Workforce for the Future," *International Journal of Environmental Research and Public Health*, Vol. 14, No. 12, December 2017.

Magill, Kate, and Edwin Lopez, "The Top Technologies Creating a 'Revolutionary Stage' in Supply Chains," *Supply Chain Dive*, July 19, 2022.

Mallakpour, Iman, and Gabriele Villarini, "The Changing Nature of Flooding Across the Central United States," *Nature Climate Change*, Vol. 5, March 2015.

Marshall, Jennifer, Jacqueline Wiltshire, Jennifer Delva, Temitope Bello, and Anthony J. Masys, "Natural and Manmade Disasters: Vulnerable Populations," in Anthony J. Masys, Ricardo Izurieta, and Miguel Reina Ortiz, eds., *Global Health Security*, Advanced Sciences and Technologies for Security Applications, Springer, 2020.

McCreight, Robert, and Wayne Harrop, "Uncovering the Real Recovery Challenge: What Emergency Management Must Do," *Journal of Homeland Security and Emergency Management*, Vol. 16, No. 3, October 2019.

McEntire, David, "Local Emergency Management Organizations," in Havidán Rodríguez, Enrico L. Quarantelli, and Russell R. Dynes, eds., *Handbook of Disaster Research*, Springer, 2007.

Mearian, Lucas, "Maersk's TradeLens Demise Likely a Death Knell for Blockchain Consortiums," *Computerworld*, December 2, 2022.

Medina, Joanne, *Analysis of Emergency Preparedness Plans in the U.S. Jurisdictions with the Highest Rates of Homelessness*, master's thesis, University of Washington, School of Public Health, Environmental and Occupational Health Sciences, 2022.

Mehrotra, Preeti, Preeti Malani, and Prashant Yadav, "Personal Protective Equipment Shortages During COVID-19: Supply Chain–Related Causes and Mitigation Strategies," *JAMA Health Forum*, Vol. 1, No. 5, May 2020.

Mensah, Peter, Yuri Merkuryev, Eric Klavins, and Sukhvir Manak, "Supply Chain Risks Analysis of a Logging Company: Conceptual Model," *Procedia Computer Science*, Vol. 104, 2017.

Merlo, Kelsey L., Kayla C. Jones, Katrina M. Conen, Elizabeth A. Dunn, Blake L. Scott, and Jennifer Marshall, "Engaged, Overextended, or Burned Out: What Is the State of the Disaster Response Workforce?" *Journal of Emergency Management*, Vol. 19, No. 9, 2021.

Meyer, Andrea, and Dana Meyer, "Supply Chain Resilience: Restoring Business Operations After a Hurricane—Summary Report," MIT Center for Transportation and Logistics, 2018.

Miami-Dade County, *Miami-Dade County Sea Level Rise Strategy*, February 2021.

Miro, Michelle E., John Lee, Susan A. Resetar, Andrew Lauland, David Metz, Vanessa Wolf, Rahim Ali, Jay Balagna, Jason Thomas Barnosky, R. J. Briggs, Edward W. Chan, Shira H. Fischer, Quentin E. Hodgson, Jenna W. Kramer, Geoffrey Kirkwood, Chelsea Kolb, Kristin J. Leuschner, Shannon Prier, Mark Stalczynski, Patricia A. Stapleton, Scott R. Stephenson, Tobias Sytsma, Kristin Van Abel, Michael J. D. Vermeer, and Brian Wong, *Assessing Risk to National Critical Functions as a Result of Climate Change: 2023 Risk Assessment Update*, RAND Corporation, RR-A1645-8, forthcoming.

Molk, Peter, "The Government's Role in Climate Change Insurance," *Boston College Environmental Affairs Law Review*, Vol. 43, No. 2, 2016.

Morris, Lauren L., and Tracie Sempier, *A Port Management Self-Assessment: Understanding How Prepared Your Port Organization Is for a Disaster*, U.S. Department of Commerce, National Oceanic and Atmospheric Administration, Oceanic and Atmospheric Research, 2016.

Murphy, Mike, "Who Is Buying into IBM's Blockchain Dreams?" *Protocol*, March 9, 2020.

NACo—*See* National Association of Counties.

NAIC—*See* National Association of Insurance Commissioners.

National Association of Counties, "Managing Disasters at the County Level: A National Survey," March 2019.

National Association of Insurance Commissioners, "U.S. Insurance Commissioners Endorse Internationally Recognized Climate Risk Disclosure Standard for Insurance Companies," April 8, 2022.

National Flood Insurance Program, Federal Emergency Management Agency, U.S. Department of Homeland Security, *Risk Rating 2.0 Methodology and Data Sources*, January 18, 2022.

Office of Inspector General, U.S. Department of Homeland Security, *FEMA Mismanaged the Commodity Distribution Process in Response to Hurricanes Irma and Maria*, OIG-20-76, September 25, 2020.

Office of Planning Advocacy, Business Action Center, Department of State, New Jersey, "Municipal Climate Resilience Planning Guide," October 2021.

Olonilua, Oluponmile, "Equity and Justice in Hazard Mitigation," in Alessandra Jerolleman and William L. Waugh, Jr., eds., *Justice, Equity, and Emergency Management*, Vol. 25, Emerald Publishing Limited, 2022.

Pan, Xiaodan, Martin Dresner, Benny Mantin, and Jun A. Zhang, "Pre-Hurricane Consumer Stockpiling and Post-Hurricane Product Availability: Empirical Evidence from Natural Experiments," *Production and Operations Management*, Vol. 29, No. 10, October 2020.

Paul, Jomon Aliyas, and Govind Hariharan, "Location-Allocation Planning of Stockpiles for Effective Disaster Mitigation," *Annals of Operations Research*, Vol. 196, July 2012.

Phillips, Anna M., "It's California Wildfire Season. But Firefighters Say Federal Hotshot Crews Are Understaffed," *Los Angeles Times*, May 18, 2021.

Phillips, Will, "Commodity Shipments Under Threat from Low Mississippi Water Levels," *Supply Management*, October 17, 2022.

Pierce, Freddie, "The Long Haul: Midwest Flooding's Supply Chain Impact," *Supply Chain Digital*, May 17, 2020.

Planetizen, "What Is By-Right Development?" webpage, undated. As of May 18, 2023: https://www.planetizen.com/definition/right-development

Port of Long Beach, *Climate Adaptation and Coastal Resiliency Plan (CRP)*, Fall 2016.

Public Law 78-346, Servicemen's Readjustment Act of 1944, June 22, 1944.

Public Law 107-296, Homeland Security Act of 2002, November 25, 2002.

Quinton, Sophie, "Lack of Federal Firefighters Hurts California Wildfire Response," *Stateline*, July 14, 2021.

Rabb, William, "30 Years Ago Andrew Upended Florida, but Current Legal Storm May Be Worse," *Insurance Journal*, August 24, 2022.

Ramnath, Shanthi, and Will Jeziorski, "Homeowners Insurance and Climate Change," *Chicago Fed Letter*, No. 460, September 2021.

Reidmiller, David R., Christopher W. Avery, David R. Easterling, Kenneth E. Kunkel, Kristen L. M. Lewis, Thomas K. Maycock, and Brooke C. Stewart, eds., *Impacts, Risks, and Adaptation in the United States: Fourth National Climate Assessment*, Vol. II, U.S. Global Change Research Program, 2018.

Resetar, Susan A., Liisa Ecola, Rachel Liang, David M. Adamson, Christopher Forinash, Lilly Shoup, Brynn Leopold, and Zachary Zabel, *Guidebook for Multi-Agency Collaboration for Sustainability and Resilience*, American Association of State Highway and Transportation Officials, Standing Committee on Planning, February 2020.

Resilinc, "Wildfires Are Up 30% Year over Year and Wreaking Havoc on Supply Chains," blog post, June 29, 2021. As of November 6, 2022:
https://www.resilinc.com/blog/
wildfires-are-up-30-year-over-year-and-wreaking-havoc-on-supply-chains/

Roberts, Patrick S., and Kris Wernstedt, "Decision Biases and Heuristics Among Emergency Management Personnel: Just Like the Public They Manage For?" *American Review of Public Administration*, Vol. 49, No. 3, April 2019.

Rossetti, Michael A., "Potential Impacts of Climate Change on Railroads," *The Potential Impacts of Climate Change on Transportation Workshop Summary and Proceedings*, 2003.

Safo, Nova, "U.S. Fire Service Is Short Thousands of Firefighters amid Pay Raise Delay," *Marketplace*, May 10, 2022.

Savitt, Amanda, Logan Gerber-Chavez, Samantha Montano, and Tanya Corbin, "Emergency Management Pandemic Planning: An Analysis of State Emergency Plans," *Journal of Emergency Management*, Vol. 21, No. 7, 2023.

Scholz, Serena, Rebecca Composto, Kevin Inks, Zoe Dutton, and Leola Abraham, "Impact of Climate Change on Supply Chains," CNA, 2021.

Schwieterman, Joseph P., and Euan Hague, "The Rise of Cargo-Focused Hub Airports: Pandemic Year 2020," Chaddick Policy Brief, Chaddick Institute for Metropolitan Development at DePaul University, March 25, 2021.

Seltenrich, Nate, "Between Extremes: Health Effects of Heat and Cold," *Environmental Health Perspectives*, Vol. 123, No. 11, November 2015.

Sharkey, Grace, "Q&A: CargoX COO Sees TradeLens' Failure as Learning Opportunity," *FreightWaves*, December 13, 2022.

Shen, Guoqiang, Xiaoyi Yan, Long Zhou, and Zhangye Wang, "Visualizing the USA's Maritime Freight Flows Using DM, LP, and AON in GIS," *ISPRS International Journal of Geo-Information*, Vol. 9, No. 5, May 2020.

Silverman, Joel, Angie De Groot, Holly Gell, Monica Giovachino, Kristin Koch, Leslie-Anne Levy, Elizabeth Myrus, and Dawn Thomas, *Why the Emergency Management Community Should Be Concerned About Climate Change: A Discussion of the Impact of Climate Change on Selected Natural Hazards*, CNA, 2010.

Siripurapu, Anshu, and Noah Berman, "The State of U.S. Strategic Stockpiles," backgrounder, Council on Foreign Relations, last updated March 2, 2023.

Skipper, Joseph B., Joe B. Hanna, and Brian J. Gibson, "Alabama Power Response to Katrina: Managing a Severe Service Supply Chain Disruption," *Journal of the International Academy for Case Studies*, Vol. 16, No. 1, 2010.

Slay, Christy, and Kevin Dooley, *Improving Supply Chain Resilience to Manage Climate Change Risks*, Sustainability Consortium and HSBC, June 2020.

Smith, Hayley, and Brittney Mejia, "Extreme Heat Waves Are Making L.A. Firefighters Sick, Adding New Dangers to Job," *Los Angeles Times*, September 2, 2022.

Smith, Matt, "In Wake of Romaine E. coli Scare, Walmart Deploys Blockchain to Track Leafy Greens," Walmart press release, September 24, 2018.

Smythe, Tiffany C., *Assessing the Impacts of Hurricane Sandy on the Port of New York and New Jersey's Maritime Responders and Response Infrastructure*, Natural Hazards Center, Quick Response Report 238, May 31, 2013.

"Spain Plans to Ban Outdoor Work in Extreme Heat," *Washington Post*, May 10, 2023.

Sporer, Celia, "Burnout in Emergency Medical Technicians and Paramedics in the USA," *International Journal of Emergency Services*, Vol. 10, No. 3, 2021.

Sprecher, Benjamin, Ichiro Daigo, Shinsuke Murakami, Rene Kleijn, Matthijs Vos, and Gert Jan Kramer, "Framework for Resilience in Material Supply Chains, with a Case Study from the 2010 Rare Earth Crisis," *Environmental Science and Technology*, Vol. 49, No. 11, 2015.

Stanley, Ellis M., and William Lee Waugh, "Emergency Managers for the New Millennium," in Ali Farazmand, ed., *Crisis and Emergency Management: Theory and Practice*, 2nd ed., Routledge, 2014.

Sturgis, Linda A., Tiffany C. Smythe, and Andrew E. Tucci, *Port Recovery in the Aftermath of Hurricane Sandy: Improving Port Resilience in the Era of Climate Change*, Center for a New American Security, August 2014.

Sullivan, Emily, Kirby Goidel, Stephanie E. V. Brown, Paul Kellstedt, and Jennifer A. Horney, "Do Hazard Mitigation Plans Represent the Resilience Priorities of Residents in Vulnerable Texas Coastal Counties?" *Natural Hazards*, Vol. 106, April 2021.

Sweet, William V., Radley Horton, Robert E. Kopp, Allegra N. LeGrande, and Anastasia Romanou, "Sea Level Rise," in Donald J. Wuebbles, David W. Fahey, Kathy A. Hibbard, David J. Dokken, Brooke C. Stewart, and Thomas K. Maycock, eds., *Climate Science Special Report: Fourth National Climate Assessment*, Vol. I, U.S. Global Change Research Program, 2017.

Swiss Re, "In a World of Growing Risk the Insurance Industry Has a Crucial Role to Play," September 6, 2021.

Sylves, Richard T., *Disaster Policy and Politics: Emergency Management and Homeland Security*, 3rd ed., Sage, February 2019.

Task Force on Climate-Related Financial Disclosures, *Recommendations of the Task Force on Climate-Related Financial Disclosures: Final Report*, June 2017.

TCFD—*See* Task Force on Climate-Related Financial Disclosures.

Tomer, Adie, and Joseph Kane, *The Great Port Mismatch: U.S. Goods Trade and International Transportation*, Global Cities Initiative, June 2015.

U.S. Army Corps of Engineers, "U.S. Waterborne Container Traffic by Port/Waterway in 2020," *Waterborne Container Traffic*, undated.

U.S. Climate Resilience Toolkit, "Planning and Land Use," webpage, last modified May 15, 2017. As of October 23, 2023:
https://toolkit.climate.gov/topics/built-environment/planning-and-land-use

U.S. Climate Resilience Toolkit, "Ports Resilience Index," webpage, last modified June 8, 2021. As of October 23, 2023:
https://toolkit.climate.gov/tool/ports-resilience-index

U.S. Code, Title 6, Domestic Security; Chapter 1, Homeland Security Organization; Subchapter III, Science and Technology in Support of Homeland Security; Section 185, Federally Funded Research and Development Centers.

U.S. Department of Homeland Security, "Ready," homepage, last updated October 20, 2023. As of July 18, 2023:
https://www.ready.gov

U.S. Department of Transportation, *Supply Chain Assessment of the Transportation Industrial Base: Freight and Logistics*, February 2022.

U.S. Environmental Protection Agency, "Brownfields Road Map," webpage, last updated December 1, 2022. As of October 23, 2023:
https://www.epa.gov/brownfields/brownfields-road-map

U.S. Environmental Protection Agency, "Flood Resilience Checklist," webpage, last updated July 27, 2023. As of October 23, 2023:
https://www.epa.gov/smartgrowth/flood-resilience-checklist

U.S. Fire Administration, Federal Emergency Management Agency, U.S. Department of Homeland Security, "National Fire Department Registry Quick Facts," May 10, 2023. As of May 10, 2023:
https://apps.usfa.fema.gov/registry/summary

Vaijhala, Shalini, and James Rhodes, "Resilience Bonds: A Business-Model for Resilient Infrastructure," *Field Actions Science Reports*, Special Issue 18, 2018.

Van Houtven, George, Michael Gallaher, Jared Woollacott, and Emily Decker, *Act Now or Pay Later: The Costs of Climate Inaction for Ports and Shipping*, RTI International, March 2022.

Vilá, Olivia, Gavin Smith, Bethany Cutts, Samata Gyawali, and Samiksha Bhattarai, "Equity in FEMA Hazard Mitigation Assistance Programs: The Role of State Hazard Mitigation Officers," *Environmental Science and Policy*, Vol. 136, October 2022.

Vose, Russell S., David R. Easterling, Kenneth E. Kunkel, Allegra N. LeGrande, and Michael F. Wehner, "Temperature Changes in the United States," in Donald J. Wuebbles, David W. Fahey, Kathy A. Hibbard, David J. Dokken, Brooke C. Stewart, and Thomas K. Maycock, eds., *Climate Science Special Report: Fourth National Climate Assessment*, Vol. I, U.S. Global Change Research Program, 2017.

Waugh, William L., and Kathleen J. Tierney, *Emergency Management: Principles and Practice for Local Government*, 2nd ed., ICMA Press, 2007.

Weaver, John, Lindsey C. Harkabus, Jeffry Braun, Steven Miller, Rob Cox, John Griffith, and Rebecca J. Mazur, "An Overview of a Demographic Study of United States Emergency Managers," *Bulletin of the American Meteorological Society*, Vol. 95, No. 2, 2014.

Wells, Jeff, "Walmart Mandates Blockchain Use for Leafy Greens Suppliers," *Grocery Dive*, September 25, 2018.

Wernstedt, Kris, Patrick S. Roberts, Joseph Arvai, and Kelly Redmond, "How Emergency Management Personnel (Mis?)Interpret Forecasts," *Disasters*, Vol. 43, No. 1, January 2019.

Wigglesworth, Alex, "Hellish Fires, Low Pay, Trauma: California's Forest Service Firefighters Face a Morale Crisis," *Los Angeles Times*, June 14, 2022.

Williams, Brian D., "Understanding Where Emergency Management Gets the Knowledge to Solve the Problems They Face: Where Are We More Than 20 Years After the *IJMED* Special Edition Calls on Closing the Gap?" *International Journal of Mass Emergencies and Disasters*, Vol. 39, No. 3, November 2021.

Winston, Andrew, "Why Business Leaders Must Resist the Anti-ESG Movement," *Harvard Business Review*, April 5, 2023.

Xia, Wenyi, and Robin Lindsey, "Port Adaptation to Climate Change and Capacity Investments Under Uncertainty," *Transportation Research Part B: Methodological*, Vol. 152, October 2021.

Xiang, Tianyi, Brian J. Gerber, and Fengziu Zhang, "Language Access in Emergency and Disaster Preparedness: An Assessment of Local Government 'Whole Community' Efforts in the United States," *International Journal of Disaster Risk Reduction*, Vol. 55, March 2021.

Xie, Lynn, "Nike: A Poster Child for Climate Change?" Harvard University, Technology and Operations Management, MBA Student Perspectives, modified November 3, 2016.

Zamuda, Craig, Bryan Mignone, Dan Bilello, K. C. Hallett, Courtney Lee, Jordan Macknick, Robin Newmark, and Daniel Steinberg, *U.S. Energy Sector Vulnerabilities to Climate Change and Extreme Weather*, U.S. Department of Energy, Office of Policy and International Affairs, DOE/PI-0013, July 2013.

Zhang, Yuqiang, and Drew T. Shindell, "Costs from Labor Losses Due to Extreme Heat in the USA Attributable to Climate Change," *Climatic Change*, Vol. 164, 2021.